The
MOFFATT
NEW TESTAMENT COMMENTARY
Based on *The New Translation* by the
REV. PROFESSOR JAMES MOFFATT, D.D., LL.D., D.LITT.
and under his Editorship

THE PASTORAL EPISTLES

The Moffatt
New Testament Commentary

MATTHEW
BY THEODORE H. ROBINSON, D.D., LITT.D.

MARK
BY B. HARVIE BRANSCOMB, D.D.

LUKE
BY W. MANSON, D.D.

JOHN
BY G. H. C. MACGREGOR, D.D., D.LITT.

THE ACTS OF THE APOSTLES
BY F. J. FOAKES-JACKSON, D.D.

ROMANS
BY C. H. DODD, D.D., F.B.A.

THE JOHANNINE EPISTLES
BY C. H. DODD, D.D., F.B.A.

I CORINTHIANS
BY JAMES MOFFATT, D.D., LL.D., D.LITT.

II CORINTHIANS
BY R. H. STRACHAN, D.D.

GALATIANS
BY GEORGE S. DUNCAN, D.D., LL.D.

PHILIPPIANS
BY J. H. MICHAEL, D.D.

COLOSSIANS, PHILEMON AND EPHESIANS
BY E. F. SCOTT, D.D.

THE PASTORAL EPISTLES
BY E. F. SCOTT, D.D.

HEBREWS
BY THEODORE H. ROBINSON, D.D., LITT.D.

THE GENERAL EPISTLES
BY JAMES MOFFATT, D.D., LL.D., D.LITT.

REVELATION
BY MARTIN KIDDLE, M.A.
ASSISTED BY M. K. ROSS

In preparation

THESSALONIANS
BY WILLIAM NEIL, B.D., PH.D.

THE
PASTORAL EPISTLES

BY

E. F. SCOTT, D.D.

Professor of Biblical Theology, Union Theological Seminary
New York

LONDON : HODDER AND STOUGHTON

FIRST PUBLISHED   OCTOBER 1936
SIXTH IMPRESSION   SEPTEMBER 1948

Made and printed in Great Britain for
Hodder and Stoughton Limited by
The Camelot Press Limited
London and Southampton

EDITOR'S PREFACE

MOFFATT'S NEW TESTAMENT COMMENTARY

THE aim of this commentary is to bring out the religious meaning and message of the New Testament writings. To do this, it is needful to explain what they originally meant for the communities to which they were addressed in the first century, and this involves literary and historical criticism; otherwise, our reading becomes unintelligent. But the New Testament was the literature of the early Church, written out of faith and for faith, and no study of it is intelligent unless this aim is kept in mind. It is literature written for a religious purpose. 'These are written that ye might believe that Jesus is the Christ, the Son of God.' This is the real object of the New Testament, that Christians might believe it better, in the light of contemporary life with its intellectual and moral problems. So with any commentary upon it. Everything ought to be subordinated to the aim of elucidating the religious content, of showing how the faith was held in such and such a way by the first Christians, and of making clear what that faith was and is.

The idea of the commentary arose from a repeated demand to have my New Testament translation explained; which accounts for the fact that this translation has been adopted as a convenient basis for the commentary. But the contributors have been left free to take their own way. If they interpret the text differently, they have been at liberty to say so. Only, as a translation is in itself a partial commentary, it has often saved space to print the commentary and start from it.

As everyman has not Greek, the commentary has been written, as far as possible, for the Greekless. But it is based upon a first-hand study of the Greek original, and readers may rest assured that it represents a close reproduction of the original writers' meaning, or at any rate of what we consider that to have been. Our common aim has been to enable everyman to-day to sit where these first Christians sat, to feel the impetus and inspiration of the Christian faith as it dawned upon the minds of the communities in the first century, and thereby to realize more vividly how new and lasting is the message which prompted these New Testament writings to take shape as they did. Sometimes people inside as well as outside the Church make mistakes about the New Testament. They think it means this or that, whereas its words frequently mean something very different from what traditional associations suggest. The saving thing is to let the New Testament speak for itself. This is our desire and plan in the present commentary, to place each writing or group of writings in its original setting, and allow their words to come home thus to the imagination and conscience of everyman to-day.

The general form of the commentary is to provide a running comment on the text, instead of one broken up into separate verses. But within these limits, each contributor has been left free. Thus, to comment on a gospel requires a method which is not precisely the same as that necessitated by commenting on an epistle. Still, the variety of treatment ought not to interfere with the uniformity of aim and form. Our principle has been that nothing mattered, so long as the reader could understand what he was reading in the text of the new testament.

JAMES MOFFATT.

CONTENTS

INTRODUCTION

COMMENTARY

CONTENTS

CONTENTS

INTRODUCTION

INTRODUCTION

I. NAME AND CHARACTER

THE Epistles to Timothy and Titus form a group by themselves within the New Testament, and need to be viewed together. They are in full agreement in their religious and ethical teaching. They have the same peculiarities of language. They deal with the same problems, occasionally in the same words. In all of them the elder apostle writes to his assistants, offering them directions for their work in the Christian mission during his absence. Since the early part of the eighteenth century the three writings have been known as the Pastoral Epistles; and the name aptly describes their common character.

It has to be admitted that these Epistles, which have come down to us as Pauline, are not on the same level as Paul's other letters. They show little of his power of thought and expression, of his insight into Christian principles, of his depth and originality. Yet they have qualities of their own which fully entitle them to their place in the New Testament, and in their practical influence they have been among the most important of all the writings. They have moulded the organization, the ethical teaching, and to no small extent the religion of the historical Church.

II. BIOGRAPHICAL SETTING

In the course of his missionary travels Paul must frequently have communicated by letter with his various assistants. Such letters, for the most part, would be confidential in their nature, or would deal briefly, in business-like style, with immediate plans and movements, and they would not find their way into Christian literature, like the elaborate letters which were addressed to churches. The Pastoral Epistles have come to us as part of this more personal correspondence. I Timothy purports to have been written after Paul had left Ephesus for Macedonia ; he hopes very shortly to rejoin Timothy in Ephesus, but meanwhile writes him a letter, impressing on him counsels which he had given by word of mouth before his departure. In the Epistle to Titus he writes to the trusted colleague whom he has left behind in Crete ; along with Titus he had planted the gospel in that island, and, after returning to the Greek mainland, sends his detailed instructions as to how the new churches should be organized. The situation in 2 Timothy is of a different kind. Paul is now aware that his own career is finished. He is a prisoner at Rome, on the eve of martyrdom, and appoints Timothy to be his successor. He has few specific instructions to offer ; his chief anxiety is that Timothy should continue his work in his own spirit, maintaining, in face of all efforts to pervert it, the gospel which he had taught. This anxiety, although it comes to its clearest expression in 2 Timothy, is also apparent in the other two Epistles.

III. AUTHENTICITY

The first New Testament Canon, drawn up by Marcion in the middle of the second century, did not include the letters to Timothy and Titus. This in itself is no argument against their genuineness, for the heretic Marcion would naturally discard these writings, in which heresy is strongly denounced. But the fact that they were excluded, at so early a date, from the body of Paul's letters, affords ground for suspicion. Could Marcion have passed them over if they were already accepted by the whole Church as the undoubted work of Paul ? The critical investigation of the last century has tended more and more to confirm the judgment of Marcion. Attempts are still made to defend the Pauline authorship of the Pastoral Epistles, but all the lines of evidence would seem to converge on a negative conclusion.

That Paul cannot have been the author is most clearly

apparent when we examine the historical framework of the letters. In Paul's life, as we know it from the book of Acts, and from the Epistles which were certainly written by him, no place can be found for the circumstances which are assumed in the Pastorals. To be sure, the narrative in Acts is only a sketch, and has little to say about some of the most important periods of Paul's career ; yet the other Epistles can all be fitted, without difficulty, into the scheme of Acts, while the Pastorals conflict with it. They are no less at variance with the data of the accepted letters—so much so that they cannot be inserted at any point in the known life of Paul without throwing everything into confusion. This is apparent when we look at the situation in each of the three letters.

1 Timothy is written from Macedonia to Timothy, who had stayed behind in Ephesus. We are told, however, of only one journey of Paul from Ephesus to Macedonia (Acts xx. 1 ; 2 Cor. ii. 13), and on that occasion he sent on Timothy before him, and joined him in Macedonia (2 Cor. i. 1). It is conceivable that during his three years' residence at Ephesus he paid a visit to Macedonia which has not been recorded ; but if so it must have come so early in the Ephesian period that the conditions indicated in 1 Timothy could not have arisen. The Epistle, for instance, deals with a church which is now mature and fully organized, not with one that has been newly founded. It deals, too, with an alarming growth of heresy in the Ephesian Church, while this was still in the future when Paul, several years afterwards, bade farewell to the elders at Miletus (Acts xx. 29).

As for the Epistle to Titus, there is no mention in Acts of a mission of Paul in Crete, and it is hard to see how a place can be found for such an episode. During the eighteen months that he worked at Corinth Paul may have crossed to the island. which was not far distant ; but the mission at Corinth made full demands on him, and he cannot have interrupted it for more than a flying visit to any other field. The Epistle to Titus assumes that he had been in Crete for a considerable time— long enough for churches to be founded in many cities (Titus i. 5), and to become infected with heresies (i. 9f.). One point is decisive against even the briefest visit to Crete in this period. It is implied in Titus iii. 13 that Apollos was now an active Christian worker, and he was not converted until a time subsequent to Paul's departure from Corinth (Acts xviii. 24f.). We have definite knowledge of only one occasion when Paul touched the island of Crete, and that was during the voyage to Italy, when the ship found temporary refuge at a place called Fair Havens (Acts xxvii. 7, 8). The captain was then waiting anxiously for a change of wind which would enable him to continue his voyage, and probably allowed no one to land. He certainly would not hold back the ship until one of his prisoners had completed a missionary tour of the island.

It is only in 2 Timothy that we have clear information as to the time and place of writing. Rome, to be sure, is only mentioned incidentally (i. 17), but it forms the background of the whole Epistle, which is written from prison, on the very eve of Paul's death (iv. 16). In this farewell letter Timothy is told, apparently for the first time, of events which must have happened five or six years before. Paul had left his cloak at Troas; Erastus had remained at Corinth; Trophimus had fallen sick at Miletus. These notices cannot be reconciled with the circumstances of the letter, and are best regarded as fragments of earlier letters which have been incorporated in the present one. But a suspicion is thus awakened that the whole Epistle, as we now have it, is an artificial composition which cannot be fitted, any more than 1 Timothy and Titus, into the actual framework of Paul's life.

It is now granted, even by those who uphold the traditional view, that if Paul wrote the Epistles they must be assigned to a period which lies quite outside of the record in Acts. A belief was current, at least as early as the time of Eusebius (about A.D. 300), that Paul's appeal to Caesar resulted in an acquittal, after which he resumed his missionary work, but was re-arrested, brought back to Rome, and condemned to death. Since the interval between the two trials is wholly dark, we are free to fill it in with any itinerary we please, and all the riddles of the Pastorals can thus be explained. But the theory of an extra period in the life of Paul is more than doubtful. It has no support except from several vague allusions by early Fathers, who probably derived their evidence from the Pastoral Epistles themselves. From the outset it was recognized that if Paul wrote them he must have done so at a stage of his career of which nothing was known. If there was an unrecorded period of this kind it could only be placed near the very end, after the time when he had faced his trial at Rome.

Our records are silent as to the outcome of Paul's trial, and for all that we certainly know he was set free, and entered on a further mission. Yet all the indications are against this conjecture. The book of Acts, although it says nothing of a condemnation, at least suggests it when it describes the sorrow of the Ephesian elders ' because they would see his face no more ' (Acts xx. 38). An even plainer suggestion is conveyed by the abrupt close of the book. One of the main objects of the author of Acts is to show that while Paul was opposed by the Jews he was consistently favoured by the Roman authorities ; and an acquittal by the emperor's court would have furnished the crowning proof of this thesis. Yet the book significantly closes just at the point when Paul is about to stand his trial. Apart from these positive evidences that the appeal to Caesar ended in disaster, we have to reckon with the fact that Paul disappears from Christian history after his arrival at Rome. If he had resumed his activity he would surely have left some trace, especially as he had now become, without any question, the outstanding figure in the Christian world. Nothing in Napoleon's career has been so vividly remembered as the hundred days after his return from Elba. Paul's escape from Rome, and the events that followed it, would have left something of a like impression on the memory of the Church.

Even if a case could be made out for an interval between two imprisonments the authenticity of the Pastorals would still be doubtful. We know, for one thing, that it was Paul's intention to proceed from Rome to Spain (Rom. xv. 24) ; yet these Epistles describe him as continuing his work in the East. Again, we should need to assume, on the ground of the Pastorals, that his interval of freedom lasted a considerable time. He must have journeyed from Rome to Ephesus, worked there along with Timothy, travelled in Greece, and returned to Ephesus, carried out an extended mission in Crete, passed over again into Greece, and perhaps spent a winter in Nicopolis. This period of renewed activity would be almost as prolonged as that of the earlier mission, and, on the theory of a second imprisonment, he enjoyed only a brief respite. Again, while the Pastorals are in conflict with the book of Acts, they give a parallel account of Paul's movements. It is impossible not to feel that the one record is dependent on the other. We read in Acts of journeys from Ephesus to Macedonia, from Corinth by way of Troas and Miletus ; and in the Pastorals the same routes are followed. Paul's companions and fellow-workers are the same as in Acts. The apostle, whose pride it was to be always breaking new ground for the gospel, would not have repeated himself in this aimless way. It is remarkable, too, that nowhere in the Pastorals does he make any reference to a long imprisonment from which he has just escaped, and which might shortly be renewed. Alike in 1 Timothy and Titus he writes as a man who has always been master of his own movements, and makes confident plans for the future. In 2 Timothy he dwells on his past sufferings, but never alludes to that recent one which had been the most terrible of all. How is this silence to be accounted for ? The most natural explanation is that the writer knows nothing of a second Roman imprisonment. He takes for granted that Paul's career has been fully covered by the narrative in the book of Acts.

It has been necessary to consider the historical data with some fulness, since any positive conclusion as to authorship must rest on them. We know too little of Paul or of the Church of his time to say of any writing ascribed to him that by intrinsic signs it cannot be his work. If the Pastorals are different in a number of ways from the other Epistles, it is always possible to argue that in his later days Paul had changed his mode of writing, that he had adapted his mission-ary methods to new circumstances, or that conditions prevailed even in his lifetime, which we might not infer from our other evidence. Arguments of this kind have often been urged, very forcibly, in defence of his authorship of the Pastorals. But in view of the difficulty, on purely historical grounds, of assigning them to Paul, full weight must be given to the other considerations which make them doubtful.

(i) The theological position is not that of Paul. It is true that Pauline phrases and conceptions are freely employed, and in a passage like Titus iii. 5–7 the cardinal Pauline doctrines are declared to be the necessary foundation of all Christian teaching. But this manifest desire of the writer to think like Paul makes his failure more significant. At almost every point he has misunderstood Paul's teaching. He does not know what Paul meant by the Law (cf. I Tim. i. 8–10) ; he confuses Pauline faith with loyalty to a Church tradition ; he forgets the central value which Paul attached to the Cross ; he has nothing to say of the conflict between flesh and Spirit ; his thought is quite untouched by the Pauline mysticism. We cannot but feel that the mind at work in these Epistles is different, in its whole bent and outlook, from that of Paul.

(ii) The language of the Epistles is not Pauline. This is apparent even in the English translation, where every careful reader will note words and phrases which are never used in the other Epistles. When the Greek is examined in detail it reveals a large number of differences, both in grammar and vocabulary, from the normal Greek of the New Testament. The reason of this may be, as has sometimes been contended, that in dealing with new subjects Paul found it necessary to write in a new style. But the peculiarities of diction are by no means confined to the treatment of matters which had now presented themselves for the first time. Again and again the familiar Pauline ideas are expressed in a manner which is quite foreign to Paul as we know him in the other Epistles. The difference, moreover, is one that suggests not merely two writers but two periods. It might be compared to the difference which everyone can detect between the English of the eighteenth and that of the nineteenth century.

(iii) The ecclesiastical conditions which are taken for granted in these Epistles are not those of Paul's lifetime. The struggling communities of Paul's day are now firmly established. Each of them is governed by a board of ' elders ' or ' bishops,' assisted by ' deacons.' For works of charity and the supervision of its female members the Church employs a staff of ' widows,' who are apparently paid for their services. In its worship and beliefs, as in its organization, the Church now aims at uniformity. In place of the simple confession ' Jesus is Lord ' there are stated formulae, in which we can trace the beginning of a creed. Orthodoxy has become the necessary mark of a good Christian.

Thus from the character of the Epistles as well as from their historical setting we may infer that they were not written by Paul ; but there is reason to qualify this conclusion. Here and there, especially in 2 Timothy, we come on passages which bear the stamp of Pauline authorship. In their style and vocabulary they conform exactly to Paul's manner ; they contain names and allusions which would not have occurred to a later inventor ; above all, they do not fit in with the context in which they are inserted. In 2 Timothy, for instance, Paul is supposed to be writing his farewell letter, and this idea that the great apostle is now on the very eve of his death is carried through, almost to the close, with singular pathos and beauty. Yet immediately after the solemn passage in which he declares that he has now finished his course, Paul summons Timothy to come to him from Ephesus. He forgets that he is to die, perhaps next day, and looks forward to his friend's arrival, in a few months' time, bringing a cloak which will keep him warm through the coming winter. It is surely impossible that the author of the previous chapters can have written this passage. He includes it because it is a genuine note of Paul for which he is anxious to find a place, even though it conflicts with what he has just written.

Here, it may be conjectured, is the key to the origin of these Pastoral Epistles. Some brief writings of Paul, addressed, most likely, to Timothy and Titus, have fallen into the hands of a later teacher. They had no value in themselves, and were mere personal notes, such as Paul must frequently have written when arranging missionary tours with his assistants. Using these fragments as a nucleus, the later writer has composed the present Epistles, which he issues in the name of Paul, since they not only give effect to Paul's teaching, but contain at least some elements of Pauline material.

IV. Date and Mutual Relation

The date of the Pastorals cannot be fixed with any precision. If the writer had come into possession of stray notes by Paul, he must have lived at a time not very far removed from that of the apostle. Besides the Pauline notes, he apparently had access to some genuine reminiscences. A number of persons are mentioned whose names were still familiar—Hymenaeus and Alexander, Philetus, Hermogenes. The accounts of Timothy's family (2 Tim. i. 5) and of the mission of Titus in Crete may well go back to good tradition. Other indications point likewise to a date comparatively early. The Church for which the Epistles were written was not the Church of Paul's day, but neither was it the complex organization which had grown up in the later part of the second century. Government and creeds and forms of worship were still of a primitive nature. No sharp line had been drawn, as in the later period, between heresy and orthodox belief. Relations with the State, though delicate, were not acutely strained. The Epistles, indeed, would seem to have been written for the very purpose of making a bridge between the Apostolic Church and the later one. In face of new developments the writer is anxious to preserve continuity with the earlier type of religion which was now being left behind. External evidence appears to confirm the dating which is suggested by the Epistles themselves. In their general outlook they are in striking agreement with the Epistle of Clement, which belongs to the closing years of the first century. Some of their characteristic terms are found in Ignatius (A.D. 116). They are quoted, in all probability, by Polycarp, the younger contemporary of Ignatius, and certainly by Justin, about twenty years later. We cannot be far wrong in concluding that they were written in the first quarter of the second century, and most likely in its early years.

A question arises as to whether all the three Epistles are by the same author. It cannot be doubted that they depend on each other, and were composed about the same time, with the same object, in the same environment. The natural inference is that they are the work of the same man. We must allow, however, for some interval between the several letters, and for some changes of attitude. In 1 Timothy the writer is chiefly concerned with Church administration ; in Titus with the need for right doctrine ; in 2 Timothy with Christian life and character. From a number of indications it may be gathered that 2 Timothy is the earliest of the three letters. It has more freshness and power than the other two ; it is richer in what seems to be authentic Pauline material ; it expresses in a more original form ideas and phrases which reappear in 1 Timothy and Titus. The inference may be drawn that a teacher who had secured some fragments of Paul's correspondence made them the basis of an Epistle in which Paul, before his death, offered counsel to his successor. At a later time he added two Epistles of the same kind. Little that was really from Paul's hand now remained to him, but again he expressed his mind on urgent questions of the day by means of letters addressed by Paul to his assistants. Of these two other letters 1 Timothy is the more elaborate, and anticipates most of the themes which are dealt with in Titus. It may be that Titus was added with a view to special difficulties which had arisen in the island of Crete.

V. General Purpose

The main purpose of the Epistles is plainly suggested by their attribution to Paul. Their author is a fervent admirer of the great apostle, in whom he sees the ideal teacher and the representative Christian man. One of the ever-recurring phrases in the Epistles is ' the healthy teaching.' It denotes the normal and authentic Christian message, free from all infection of wrong belief and practice. Paul had taught and exemplified this true Christianity, and had left it to his successors as a ' deposit ' which had to be guarded faithfully.

So the aim of the writer is to secure that the Pauline tradition should be maintained. He lived in a time when the Church was changing its character. It was no longer a free brotherhood, detached from worldly interests, but an organization, which had to hold its own within the social structure of the day. It was largely composed of converts who had brought in with them the moral standards of paganism. It was affected by contemporary movements, and Christian ideas were being mingled with strange speculations which were often alien to the whole spirit of the gospel. Was it not possible, under the new conditions, to preserve Christianity in its purity ? This could only be done, in the writer's view, by holding fast to Paul's instructions, alike in matters of doctrine and of practical Christian living. If the Church was to survive, and accomplish its destined work, it must be built up deliberately on the Pauline foundation. It has to be admitted that this disciple of Paul has failed, in not a few respects, to understand him ; by his very insistence on fidelity to the Pauline tradition he has broken with Paul, for whom the energy of the living Spirit had taken the place of every tradition. Yet in the main he has succeeded in his object. He takes the ideas which Paul had made fundamental and gives them a permanent place in the creed of the Church. He makes it plain, as Paul had done, that faith is useless unless it manifests itself in Christian living. It has often been objected that he transforms the passionate apostle into a sober-minded churchman, dispensing counsels which can sometimes be hardly distinguished from worldly wisdom. But even here he shows a real insight, for Paul, with all his enthusiasm, was sane and practical, and took due account of given conditions. It meant everything for the future of the Church that Paul found an interpreter who at least did justice to his common sense.

The Pastorals are written, then, in the interest of the Pauline tradition. In 2 Timothy, Paul the man is held up as the pattern for all true Christians. In 1 Timothy and Titus it is Paul the teacher to whom the Church is directed for guidance. Difficulties were confronting it which had not been foreseen in the earlier days of the mission, but this writer sees a way by which they can be overcome ; he goes back to Paul and recalls what he had taught, and tries to realize how he would act and advise in the new situation. If the Church is to find its bearings amidst the present confusion it must look to Paul. But this general aim of re-establishing the Pauline tradition involves several others, of a more specific nature, which need to be considered separately.

VI. Ecclesiastical Purpose

Towards the end of the first century the Church had developed as an institution, under official leaders. It had consisted, in the primitive age, of a number of small communities, the members of which were theoretically on an equal footing, all of them possessed of the Spirit, which took the place of any outward control. In each community there were men who had charge of the ordinary routine, while travelling apostles paid occasional visits and exercised a vague supervision ; but this ministry was in no sense official. At a later time, as the Church increased in numbers and the duties became ever more complicated, the early system was found to be unworkable. The community in each city had now its regular staff of duly appointed officers, some of whom gave their whole time to the work. Everything now depended on these governing men. It was they who guarded the Church's doctrine, who upheld its moral standards, who represented it in face of a hostile world. The writer of the Pastorals is concerned not so much with the Church at large as with its responsible leaders.

From this it has generally been inferred that the Epistles were meant to form a manual of Church order, similar to others which have come down to us from the early centuries. It is held that Paul himself, or an unknown teacher some fifty years after his death, devised a constitution for the Church; he set up a hierarchy of officials and prescribed the rules which were to guide them in their various functions. This view, however, is not borne out by closer examination of the Epistles. In 2 Timothy the question of organization is hardly touched on. In 1 Timothy it is only discussed in two passages (iii. 1–13; v. 17–22), to which may possibly be added the section on Widows (v. 3–16). In Titus the official ministry is only dealt with in a few verses (i. 5–9) which repeat the injunctions of 1 Tim. iii. 1–13 in a briefer form. Thus all that is said of organization is comprised in something like a tenth part of the Epistles, and even in this there is nothing that can properly be called Church order. It is taken for granted that a government by elders and deacons is already established, and the writer's one anxiety is that it should be entrusted to the right men. He has nothing to say about the ecclesiastical duties which they will be required to perform. They receive no instructions as to the conduct of worship, the administration of sacraments, the management of finance, the extension of Christian work, or the relations with civil authorities. All the counsels are quite general in their nature, and have far more to do with personal character than with any technical qualifications. Manuals of Church order consist entirely of definite rules for discipline and organization ; this is what we expect of them, and everything else is out of place. This writer demands nothing of elders and deacons except that they should be good men who will worthily represent the Church. So far from being an ecclesiastic, solely intent on rules and forms, he seems hardly to be interested in such things at all. He constantly declares, almost in so many words, that it is not the system which matters but the men. The section on Widows (1 Tim. v. 3–16) comes nearer than any other to the style of a Church manual. A subject of minor importance is here treated at disproportionate length, and in something like the manner of a code-book. It may be that the writer feels the need of regulating this part of the Church's ministry, or that he quotes some rules already in existence which have fallen into neglect. But even in this section his interest is not in the mere official arrangements ; he is anxious that the Church should not be compromised by its female workers, and lays much more stress on the character and behaviour of the widows than on their special duties. A chapter is indeed devoted (1 Tim. ii.) to the conduct of worship, but it contains none of the directions which we look for in an ecclesiastical manual. Nothing is said of the order of service, of the formalities to be observed, of the parts to be taken by minister and congregation. All reference to the Lord's Supper, which had by this time become the central part of worship, is strangely absent. The one question discussed is that of prayer, especially of prayer on behalf of rulers and magistrates. It is for this purpose that the whole passage seems to be inserted. Christians are to make it clear, in their meetings for worship, that they are good citizens, anxious to do all they can to promote the public welfare.

It may be concluded, then, that the Epistles contain nothing which can be called Church legislation. The writer accepts the ecclesiastical system which had now displaced the less formal one of the previous age. The communities were still independent of each other, but had developed a mechanism of local government. Each of them was controlled by elders or presbyters who were regularly ordained to office, and who acted together as a board. They were also called 'bishops'— i.e. 'overseers'—and this Greek term was now preferred to that which had been borrowed from the synagogue, though both of them are used interchangeably in these Epistles. The bishops were assisted by 'deacons,' whose duties are not specified, but had probably to do with matters of finance and ordinary business. The work of teaching was entrusted to those of the elders who were properly qualified. Women of mature years visited from house to house and attended to various charities. Both the men and the women who devoted their whole time to the affairs of the Church were paid for their work. The writer of the Epistles accepts these arrangements, and does not appear to suggest a change or an addition to any of them. His one concern is to make sure that all the duties will be performed conscientiously, by worthy men and women. It has often been held that the Epistles were written in the interest of the episcopal system, which was coming to be generally adopted in the early part of the second century. This is hardly possible, since the writer never employs the word 'bishop' as the exclusive title of one man. If there is any advocacy of the later system it is to be found, not in anything expressly said in the letters, but in the fact that they are addressed to Timothy and Titus. Paul is represented as conferring on these men a general oversight of churches, similar to that which was afterwards exercised by a diocesan bishop. But if it was intended that Timothy and Titus should be thought of as typical ' bishops,' the word would not have been used so indiscriminately to denote ordinary elders. Most likely Timothy and Titus belong merely to the dramatic setting of the Epistles. Paul is described as imparting his counsels for the benefit of the Church after him, and he addresses himself naturally to the younger assistants whom he has himself trained, and who in due course will take up his work. It is to be noted that no directions are given them as to the perpetuation of their own office. Their function is simply to serve as links between Paul and the future Church, committing what they have heard from him to faithful men, who in their turn will teach others (2 Tim. ii. 2).

VII. Doctrinal Purpose

A large place is given in all three Epistles to the condemnation of certain forms of teaching which had invaded the Church (1 Tim. i. 3–13, 19–20 ; iv. 1–18 ; vi. 3–5 ; 2 Tim. ii. 16–26 ; iii. 6–9 ; Titus i. 9–16 ; iii. 9–11). Some particular heresy is doubtless in the writer's mind, but its precise nature is hard to determine. Apparently it had some affinity to Judaism, and was concerned with ' legal controversies ' (Titus iii. 9 ; 1 Tim. i. 7f.) and those ' fables and genealogies ' which had been grafted on the Old Testament history (1 Tim. i. 7f. ; iv. 7 ; Titus i. 14). At the same time it included speculations of a pagan or gnostic character. Most probably it was akin to the heresy denounced in Colossians, in which Jewish and heathen elements were likewise mingled. Gnosticism in its later development was strongly anti-Jewish, but at the outset it seems to have welcomed Jewish ideas, and never ceased to employ Jewish material in the construction of its myths. The Pastorals take a firm stand against the encroachment of this heresy, but they cannot be described in anything but a loose sense as controversial. They make no attempt whatever to refute the false teaching ; indeed they touch on it so vaguely that we have difficulty in guessing its nature. The one definite error to which there is any allusion is ' that the resurrection has come already ' (2 Tim. ii. 18) ; and in what manner this belief was held we are not told. It is doubtful, indeed, whether the writer himself had any real acquaintance with the heresy which he condemns. He is content to ridicule it as ' vain babbling,' ' old wives' fables,' ' a spreading cancer,' ' make-believe knowledge.' Its teachers are accused of mercenary motives, and are compared to the Egyptian sorcerers who counterfeited the works of Moses and were put to shame. All this is in the style of the modern orator who denounces communism or spiritualism or some other delusion of the day. He has never troubled to make a study of these subjects, and in this he may show wisdom. But his invective cannot be accepted as argument.

The writer does not pretend to discuss the heresy, and Timothy is expressly warned against taking it seriously and so entangling himself in ' foolish, ill-mannered controversies which engender strife.' Error must be counteracted by positive assertion of the genuine Christian beliefs. To insist on these, in opposition to all forms of false teaching, is one of the chief objects of the Pastoral Epistles.

In a number of passages the writer sums up, in succinct fashion, the elements of ' sound doctrine,' and is careful to repeat the ideas and, as far as possible, the very language of Paul (cf. I Tim. vi. 11–16, iii. 16 ; 2 Tim. i. 8–10, ii. 11–14 ; Titus ii. 11–14, iii. 5–7). He declares that Christ gave Himself for our redemption, that we are justified not by our own righteousness but by faith in Christ, that God called us by His grace before the world was, and that we are destined to an eternal life on which we can enter even now. These are no mere perfunctory echoes of Pauline thought. For this writer, as for Paul himself, Christianity is the ' Truth,' immediately revealed by God, and he thinks of right belief as absolutely vital. At the same time his religious attitude is different

xxx

from that of Paul, and comes out in the characteristic word *eusebeia* on which all the teaching of the Epistles may be said to turn. It means literally ' piety,' but perhaps is most adequately rendered by the old word ' godliness.' The Christian, in this writer's view, is one who lives for God and carries with him, in all that he does, the consciousness of God. He is contrasted with the ' profane ' man—that is, the materialist, for whom spiritual things mean nothing. When the various passages are brought together, this godliness which marks the Christian would seem to involve two things ; on the one hand a right belief, on the other hand a right mode of action. In ordinary Greek the word is specially applied to the man who is careful in his observance of all the prescribed rites of religion ; and it also carries something of this shade of meaning in the Pastorals. Holding the right belief, the godly man combines it with the right kind of service, both to God and to his fellow-men.

A difference is here apparent between the religion of the Pastorals and that of Paul. In the teaching of Paul (and this is likewise true of Jesus' own teaching), faith and action are inseparable. The good life is nothing but the ' fruit,' the natural outcome, of faith. Through his new relation to God the will of God takes possession of the believer, and he acts by it almost without his knowing. In the Pastorals faith is not so much a root as a foundation (cf. I Tim. iii. 15 ; vi. 19)— the necessary basis of all right living, though it does not of itself produce it. Paul's conception of grace undergoes a similar change. While the writer thinks of salvation as the free gift of God he allows for a co-operation on the part of men. He describes grace as acting by a process of education (Titus ii. 11, 12). Through the grace bestowed on us in the gift of Christ we are enabled to master all lower desires and follow the way of godliness.

Religion, therefore, as this writer understands it, consists of two elements, which are themselves separate although in the true Christian they are joined together. For this reason it has often been felt that the Epistles have little religious value ; they are the work of a moralist to whom faith is something extraneous, a matter of orthodoxy rather than of living apprehension of God. This impression is certainly wrong. The writer has not succeeded like Paul in fusing his faith and his ethics, but faith is cardinal for him as it is for Paul. If it is not the spring, it is at least the essential condition of morality. The Christian holds to certain beliefs as eternally true, and is thus enabled to live the Christian life with entire confidence. If religion is for Paul a power working within the man, it is for this writer the solid ground beneath his feet. In the last resort it is nothing but this conviction that life must be based on religion, which gives meaning to the Pastoral Epistles.

VIII. ETHICAL PURPOSE

It was inevitable that in letters intended for Christian leaders in their work of practical oversight, the discussion should mainly turn on questions of moral conduct. The Pastoral Epistles are different from the undoubted writings of Paul, not because their interest is chiefly ethical, but because they teach an ethic which, in some respects, is not that of Paul. The distinction, to state it in the broadest terms, is this. Paul's ethic is a purely Christian one ; he insists that action must spring directly from the impulse of the Spirit, and otherwise loses all moral worth : ' Whatever is not of faith is sin ' (Rom. xiv. 23). The author of the Pastorals thinks of morality as something by itself. Only the Christian can attain to the right life, since he has the gospel teaching and the scriptures and the examples of faithful men to guide him. But it lies with himself to make use of all the light he has and so to discover the right path. Our author, therefore, approaches all moral problems with a certain detachment. He does not rely, like Paul, on the simple direction of the Spirit, but considers deliberately how men ought to arrange their lives. He takes account not only of what is most Christian but of what is seemly, prudent, useful, agreeable to settled custom. Again and again we have the sense of alien factors in his ethical teaching. His aim is to recall the moral standards of Paul to an age that is falling away from them ; but he himself appears to blend the older precepts with others of a different order.

It has to be admitted that this moral uncertainty is due, in large measure, to the separation of action from faith. When Christian behaviour had ceased to grow spontaneously out of Christian beliefs it came to be construed externally. The writer of the Pastorals requires to think out his rules for right living, and makes use of all kinds of material in forming his judgment. His attitude often impresses us as one of compromise rather than of consistent principle. At the same time this attitude is, in some degree, taken deliberately. Since the days of Paul the situation of the Church had changed, and while the Pauline rule of life is in substance preserved it is adapted to the new requirements.

For one thing, the hope of an immediate return of Christ had now fallen into the background. It still had its place in Christian belief, as it has to this day, and it finds expression more than once in these Epistles. But it was no longer a determining motive in the life of Christians, as when Paul advised his converts not to change their condition, since the time was so short as to make this unnecessary (1 Cor. vii. 20f, 29–31). It had now become evident that the Church must prepare itself for an indefinite time of waiting, and must aim at some adjustment between its heavenly calling and the earthly environment in which it must remain.

Again, since the time of Paul the Church had gathered into its fold a great number of members, of very miscellaneous character. It could no longer be assumed that Christians were an elect race, wholly absorbed in the higher interests. For the most part they were ordinary men and women, sharing in the common pursuits, though accepting the law of Christ. If this law was to be anything but an abstract ideal, it had to be presented in such a manner as to bring it within the reach of all. The absolute demands had to be qualified if they were to be fully practical.

Once more, Christianity had now identified itself with the Gentile world. Its religious message had already been thrown into the moulds of Greek thought, and its moral teaching had likewise to be re-interpreted. The Greeks had developed an ethic, in many ways a lofty one, and the effort was made to combine it with that of the gospel. Paul himself had expressed some elements of Christian morals in the current terms of Stoicism, and in the Pastorals this Hellenizing process is carried further. This is most clearly apparent in the emphasis laid on the two requirements of moderation and self-control. According to Greek teachers virtue consists in observing the middle path between two extremes, and this can be achieved only by mastery over the passions, which drive men constantly to one side or the other. The writer of the Pastorals makes no direct reference to the Golden Mean, but we can feel everywhere that he accepts it as a guiding principle. All fanaticism is abhorrent to him. Like the Greek moralists he is impatient even of virtues when they are pushed too far. He recognizes that the good things of life were meant to be enjoyed. There must be no ban on marriage, or on particular kinds of food, or even on the use of wine, since these are the gifts of God. The love of riches is condemned, but it is assumed that if a man has riches he is entitled to use them, so long as he does so for some good purpose. To the Greek influence we may also ascribe the importance attached to outward demeanour. The Christian, and especially the Christian leader, must behave himself with dignity. He must be careful in his speech and manner, and never be inveigled into vulgar brawls. Christian women are to dress quietly and be modest in their bearing and keep aloof from all scandalous talk. One feels at times that with this writer the appearance is hardly less imperative than the inward grace.

But while the Epistles allow for compromise it cannot be said that they teach an easy morality. Nowhere in the New Testament is the heroic note so unmistakably sounded. Paul is put forward as the great example because he was the soldier of Christ and died in the good fight. The principle is laid down as self-evident that all who follow godliness must endure persecution (2 Tim. iii. 12). Not infrequently the effect of blending the Christian ethic with the Greek is to make it more difficult. The follower of Christ must not only suffer passively, but must aim at a vigorous self-control. He must take his part in this world, and thereby engage in valiant struggle with its temptations. It must be noted, too, that the writer's whole purpose, when he seems to lower the Christian rule, is to make sure that it will be honestly practised. An ideal that is too high for human nature ceases to be taken seriously, and some kind of sentimentalism will by and by take the place of action. This writer calls for virtues which everyone may achieve if he sincerely tries, and if one does not make the effort he stands self-condemned.

IX. Historical Value

From a historical point of view the Epistles are of the highest importance. More than any other documents they light up for us that age succeeding the death of Paul when the Church, as we still know it, was taking definite shape. Institutions and practices were being reduced to system. Beliefs were coming to crystallize themselves in a stated creed. The scattered communities, though not yet federated, were assuming a uniform character. The Pastoral Epistles have come to us from that time when the Catholic Church was in process of formation. They were not intended to furnish a code of ecclesiastical law, but the view that would so regard them is in a broad sense justified. Unconsciously in that time of transition the Church was drawing up its programme for the future.

The Epistles are of historical value not only for their own age, but for that which had gone before. Although Paul did not write them, they doubtless preserve some authentic memories of the apostle and the men who had worked with him as well as of the movements in which he had played his part. Above all, they give us an impression of the man himself as he appeared in retrospect. In his lifetime it had been impossible to judge him except from a party point of view, but after his death, when jealousies and controversies had died down, he stood out as indubitably the greatest of the apostles. The Church could set before it no higher aim than to keep faithful to his teaching and example.

The Epistles are of cardinal value for the study of the New Testament itself. The writer is well acquainted with the extant letters of Paul, and particularly with Romans, Galatians, 1 Corinthians, and Philippians. He was also familiar with the book of Acts, from which he borrows most of his data for the setting of First and Second Timothy. He apparently knows First Peter and the Epistle to the Hebrews. In view of a number of close resemblances it is more than likely that he had read our Synoptic Gospels, and especially the Gospel of Luke. If he wrote in the early years of the second century these New Testament books must already have existed long enough to become generally accessible. One remarkable feature of the three Epistles is their use of Christian documents which are not included in our New Testament. A special interest attaches to the ' faithful sayings,' which are evidently quotations from some source with which everyone was familiar. For the most part they are lyrical in form, and may be fragments of hymns or of liturgical confessions, intended for singing or chanting. Apart from the ' sayings,' several of the doxologies have little relation to their context, and are probably taken from a liturgy.

X. PERMANENT VALUE

The Epistles have much more than an historical importance, and it is in some ways unfortunate that a writer who had himself a distinctive message should have chosen to conceal himself under the name of Paul. He employed a device which was well understood in the ancient world, and which was the more permissible if he based the Epistles, as is more than probable, on genuine notes of Paul. Yet the effort to imitate Paul gives an air of artificiality to his writing, and prevents him from uttering freely what was in his own mind. It has meant a loss to ourselves, since it keeps us in ignorance of a teacher who, in his own right, would have been well worth knowing. He was clearly a man of broad outlook and singular sagacity, and a shrewd observer of human nature. The types which he describes, often in two or three incisive words, are still to be recognized—pretentious intellectuals with their 'empty babble,' silly women who pass from one cult to another in search of a new thrill, members of the Church who use piety as a means of gain, who saddle the community with their personal duties, who carry right practices to a foolish excess. It is surprising how many of the difficulties which arise in Church life to-day have been anticipated by this writer, and how often his directions are still helpful. All through its history the Church has owed an incalculable debt to these Epistles, which have lent scriptural authority to wise and practical counsels.

The sobriety of their teaching has often been felt to detract from their religious value. As we turn to them from the Fourth Gospel and the writings of Paul we seem to descend into a less spiritual atmosphere. The writer has almost nothing to say about the inner life ; he never appears to realize the absolute nature of the Christian demands. All that he insists on is right belief, courage and loyalty and uprightness, seemly behaviour, honourable fulfilment of all obligations. He has been accused by some modern critics of substituting a 'bourgeois religion' for the authentic gospel. It is just here, however, that we can perceive the lasting service which he rendered to Christianity. He wrote in the time when the first wave of enthusiasm had spent itself. It was now apparent that the Lord would not return in a few weeks or months to bring in His Kingdom. If the Church was to survive it must transform itself into an organized society, and make terms with earthly conditions which would endure, perhaps, for ages to come ; it must make room for all sorts of people, and educate them patiently in that higher life which for most of them had little meaning. How was the Church to fit itself into the present world and still be the 'household of God' ? How was the Christian message to be made available to common humanity ? This is the question which the author of the Pastorals sets himself to answer, and which forces itself in new forms on each generation. It must always be answered by some kind of compromise, for Christianity, in its ultimate demand, is a religion for the elect few, and they have themselves been the first to confess that they fall short of it. If it is to be the world's possession—and otherwise it has failed of its purpose —it must be brought within the capacity of the general mass of men. It may be granted that from the Pastoral Epistles we should never guess what Christianity has meant to the saints and mystics. The precepts of the Gospels, the aspirations of Paul and John, are transposed into a lower key. But it may truly be said of this writer that while he compromises he does not abandon anything that is essential. He insists on the great Christian beliefs ; he allows no debasing of the moral standards ; he seeks to adapt the Church to existing conditions, but is resolute that there should be a clear distinction between the Church and the world. The religion of these Epistles may not be the highest, but in the men and women who have honestly practised it the Church in all time since has found its strength. Because he thus made Christianity a working religion for ordinary men, the author of the Pastorals may justly be ranked among the great Christian teachers.

COMMENTARY

THE FIRST EPISTLE OF PAUL THE APOSTLE
TO TIMOTHEUS

THE FIRST EPISTLE OF PAUL THE APOSTLE
TO TIMOTHEUS

i.

Paul an apostle of Christ Jesus by command of God our Saviour 1
and Christ Jesus our Hope, to Timotheus his lawful son in 2
the faith : grace, mercy, peace from God the Father and
Christ Jesus our Lord.

The salutation is so framed as to suggest a letter which is at
once personal and official. Paul writes as a father to a well-
loved son and also as an apostle who holds a Divine commission. All that he says must therefore be regarded as
authoritative. The name **Saviour** is frequently used in the 1
Epistles, and is applied both to God and Christ. In the Old
Testament it bears the quite general sense of ' rescuer ' or
' deliverer,' and this is also its meaning in the few passages
where it occurs in the earlier New Testament writings (e.g.
Phil. iii. 20 : ' we look for a saviour,' i.e. ' one who will set
us free '). At a later time the word was associated with the
Christian hope of redemption into a higher life. It was
already employed in various pagan cults to mark the divinities
who offered immortality to their worshippers, and its use in
the Pastorals may be partly due to Gentile influence. At the
same time it has not yet become the specific title of Christ.
It is God Himself who is here described as **Saviour**, since the
work of Christ depends, in the last resort, on God. Christ is
our **Hope** in the sense that He is the pledge and instrument
of our salvation, much as a great leader is said to be the
' hope ' of his country.

Several times in his Epistles Paul speaks of his converts as 2
his ' children ' (e.g. Gal. iv. 19 ; 1 Cor. iv. 15), and Timothy is
addressed emphatically as his **lawful son**—the child who most
resembles his father. He is a son ' in faith ' or in the faith ;

5

here, as elsewhere in the Pastorals, it is hard to decide whether **faith** has its strict Pauline meaning, or simply denotes the Christian religion. To Timothy, then, as to his spiritual son, Paul sends his greeting, and changes the conventional formula with which ancient letters began into a real benediction. May Timothy enjoy the **grace, mercy,** and **peace** which God bestows through Christ !

True Christianity and Error (i. 3–11)

3 As I asked you when I was on my way to Macedonia, stay where you are at Ephesus and warn certain individuals against

4 teaching novelties and studying myths and interminable genealogies ; such studies bear upon speculations rather

5 than on the divine order which belongs to faith. Whereas the aim of the Christian discipline is the love that springs from a pure heart, from a good conscience, and from a

6 sincere faith. Certain individuals have failed here by

7 turning to empty argument ; doctors of the Law is what they want to be, but they have no idea either of the meaning of the words they use or of the themes on which they

8 harp. I am well aware that ' the Law is admirable '—

9 provided that one makes a lawful use of it ; he must keep in mind that no law is ever made for honest people but for the lawless and the insubordinate, for the impious and the sinful, for the irreverent and the profane, for parricides

10 and matricides, murderers, immoral persons, sodomites,

11 kidnappers, liars, perjurers, and whatever else is contrary to sound doctrine as laid down by that glorious gospel of the blessed God with which I have been entrusted.

This passage at the beginning provides the key to all that follows. The writer, alarmed by the encroachment of alien theories and speculations, seeks to bring the Church back to the genuine Christian teaching, as it had come down from the apostle Paul. In order that the Pauline tradition may be preserved, he desires that the Church should be rightly organized. Offices are to be entrusted to dependable men ;

public worship is to be properly conducted ; the behaviour of Christian men and women is to be supervised more strictly. The life of the soul cannot maintain itself apart from the body, and if true religion is to survive it must be lodged in a well-ordered Church.

The passage consists of one long sentence, very loosely con- 3 structed and never really finished. It begins : ' As I told you before,' and this is plainly meant to lead up to some new admonition. But the writer loses himself in fresh ideas which occur to him, and only takes up the thread again in ii. 1 (' I now counsel you '). Letters often begin with some reference to the last occasion on which the two friends had met, and Timothy is reminded, at the opening of this Epistle, of how he and Paul had parted at Ephesus. As he set out for Macedonia, Paul had charged his assistant to remain in the city and combat the efforts of certain teachers who were leading the Church astray. We know of only one occasion when Paul left Ephesus for Macedonia, and Timothy had then been sent on before him (Acts xix. 22). If the reference here is to some other journey, not recorded in the book of Acts, it must have been a mere flying visit, and there would have been little purpose in the present letter, which would scarcely arrive before his return. It is suggested that Timothy had been anxious to accompany Paul, but had been advised to stay at his post and warn certain individuals against teaching novelties. The word used for this new type of teaching was possibly coined by the writer himself. He has in his mind men whom he carefully avoids naming, who professed themselves Christians but had wandered off the straight road into paths that led nowhere. The objection to their teaching is not so much its falsehood as its futility. It distracted the minds of their hearers from the great verities of the gospel to mere side-issues and puzzles. This is brought out by the reference to **myths and interminable** 4 **genealogies** and to the effect of these vain studies. Christianity, as the writer knows it, consists in the practical service of God, grounded in a true belief. These teachers have turned religion into an intellectual plaything. They spend their time in the effort to solve one curious problem and another, forgetting the one purpose for which the gospel was given. The attitude condemned is one which has been only too familiar in all ages, and which Jesus Himself denounced in His parable of the children playing in the market-place. But while the general meaning is plain, the details are difficult. In the myths and genealogies some would see an allusion to gnostic systems, with their fantastic theories of a disturbance in the heavenly world and a consequent fall of spirit into matter. These gnostic myths all turned on genealogies, emanations of one pair of aeons from another in a long series. In Titus i. 14, however, the myths are expressly defined as Jewish, and in Titus iii. 9 genealogies are conjoined with disputes about the Law. From verse 7 in the present passage we learn that the teachers in question posed as authorities on the Law, and the reference must be to some form of Jewish teaching. We know that from an early time rabbis were wont to construct fables and allegories from hints afforded by the Old Testament ; much of the popular teaching in the synagogue was of this type, and was collected at a later time in the portion of the Talmud which is known as ' Haggada.' The lists of bare names in Old Testament genealogies were easily expanded into fictitious histories, supposed to illustrate God's dealings with His people, and an example is still preserved to us in the apocalyptic Book of Jubilees. The practice, indeed, was so common that the word ' genealogy ' was often used in the sense of mythical history, and this would seem to be its meaning in the present verse. It is not unlikely that in the Judaism of the Dispersion the fables based on scripture names took on a philosophical character, which gave them a resemblance to gnostic myths. Philo, by his allegorical method, had evolved a metaphysic from the patriarchal history, and less gifted teachers would deal in much the same manner with other parts of the Old Testament. When the genealogies are called ' endless ' or interminable the reference need not be to the lengthiness of those strings of names which are found in Genesis, Nehemiah, Chronicles. It is implied, rather, that since those embroideries on scripture were wholly the product of fancy there was no reason why they should not be spun out for ever. Their effect, therefore, is only to engender **speculations**, one guess leading to another, one problem giving rise to a further one. This fruitless discussion is contrasted with the **divine order which belongs to faith.** A word is used which means literally ' economy ' or ' stewardship,' and which is sometimes applied by Paul to the Divine plan or purpose. This is the rendering preferred by Moffatt, and would convey the idea that these speculative thinkers replace God's true **order,** as revealed to faith, by one which is quite imaginary. But the contrast is between two activities, not between two views of the world. It is objected to the new teachers that by their discussions they only foster an idle curiosity, instead of a resolve to be faithful in God's service. Perhaps the Parable of the Talents was in the writer's mind when he chose a word denoting ' stewardship.'

Timothy had been left in Ephesus to lay a charge on the 5 local Church, and the aim of the charge, the result to which it will lead if duly acted on, is **love.** This moral condition, and not some fancied intellectual satisfaction, is the goal of the Christian life. The love will proceed from a threefold root— **a pure heart, a good conscience, and a sincere faith.** For Paul himself faith was sufficient, but this disciple has not fully grasped Paul's conception of faith. He thinks of it as a believing frame of mind which needs to be supplemented by a change of heart and a moral effort. It is significant that he transfers to faith the epithet which Paul applies to love. For Paul faith is a relation to God which cannot be counterfeited, while love is a relation to our fellow-men which we constantly pretend to when it is absent.

The conditions of the Christian life are plain, but ' some ' 6 have missed them by turning aside, like travellers who leave the high-road for a path that leads nowhere. As elsewhere in the Epistles this delusive by-way is described as **empty argument** or ' vain chatter.' Under this contemptuous term the writer includes all mere theorizing about religion ; since it has no moral aim it is futile, however learned and profound it may appear. From the passage which follows it would appear that some kind of Jewish teaching is in question. **They** 7 want to be doctors of the Law—that is, while professing to explain the gospel, their real interest is in Jewish controversies, and their chief ambition is to match rabbinical experts on their own ground. But, just as they are useless for Christian purposes, they also fail as rabbis, since they do not know the meaning either of **the words they use** or the things they insist on. A genuine rabbi would at once see that these Christian exponents of the Law were mere pretenders, making up by volubility for their utter ignorance of the subject. It may be gathered that the teaching at Ephesus was not only Jewish, but that it aimed in some manner at re-establishing the Law. By means of abstruse speculation a new significance was given to the ceremonial rules. Examples of the method are frequent in the Jewish Haggada : e.g. a question is raised as to why a custom, apparently meaningless, should be observed, and the answer is given in some far-fetched supernatural story. Our writer goes on to show that for the Christian this preoccupa-

8 tion with the Law is unnecessary. **The Law is admirable if** one uses it ' lawfully '—i.e. in a proper manner, and for the
9 purpose for which law is intended. This purpose is now explained. The Law was never meant for those who act rightly. It was designed as a curb on evildoers, and a number of examples are given of the sins and vices which the Law prohibits. The list follows the general lines of the decalogue. It first enumerates offences against God, and then crimes
10 against our fellow-men—murder, adultery, theft, perjury, falsehood—according to the order of the ten commandments. Extreme instances are given of each offence, to emphasize the idea that law only applies to sin in its grosser forms. From this it is argued that law has no meaning for Christians. Towards the end of the passage a phrase is introduced which plays a great part in these Pastoral Epistles, **sound doctrine** or ' healthy teaching.' As contrasted with all morbid types of belief, the gospel is healthy. It has no taint of error, but is like water fresh from the spring. As here used the phrase has a peculiar fitness. Law is a sort of medicine, only to be applied where the moral nature is diseased ; Christian teach-
11 ing is a healthy food for healthy people, a means of joy,

freedom, larger activity. The Law is useless now that we can judge good and evil according to the supreme standard, the glorious gospel of the blessed God.

Viewed as a whole this passage recalls the teaching of Galatians and Romans. Some of the familiar phrases of these Epistles are repeated (Rom. iii. 11, vii. 14, viii. 4, xiii. 8–10 ; Gal. v. 22–23), and the writer is evidently seeking to reassert Paul's conviction that by faith in Christ we are set free from the Law. Yet he has failed to apprehend Paul's meaning. He has confused the Mosaic Law with law in general, and thinks of it merely as a necessary check on evildoing. Paul, with his Jewish reverence for the Law, could never have said that it was not intended for righteous men. He had been taught to conceive of righteousness as nothing else than obedience to the Law. Even as a Christian he admits that ' the Law is holy ' (Rom. vii. 12) and that it has failed of its purpose because men with their fleshly nature could not live up to it (Rom. viii. 3) ; God had bestowed it not for the repression of evil, but as the positive means of salvation. It may be concluded from this passage alone that the present Epistle is not by Paul. In his effort to repeat Paul's criticism of the Law, the writer has laid himself open to his own stricture on the false teachers that ' they do not understand the things on which they insist.'

PAUL AS THE REPRESENTATIVE OF THE GOSPEL (i. 12–17)

I render thanks to Christ Jesus our Lord, who has made me 12 able for this ; He considered me trustworthy and appointed me to the ministry, though I had formerly been 13 a blasphemer and a persecutor and a wanton aggressor. I obtained mercy because in my unbelief I had acted out of ignorance ; and the grace of our Lord flooded my life, 14 along with the faith and love that Christ Jesus inspires. It is a sure word, it deserves all praise, that ' Christ Jesus 15 came into the world to save sinners ' ; and though I am the foremost of sinners, I obtained mercy for the purpose 16 of furnishing Christ Jesus with a supreme proof of His

17   utter patience, a typical illustration of it for all who were to believe in Him and gain eternal life. To the King of eternity, immortal, invisible, the only God, be honour and glory for ever and ever : Amen.

The previous passage has closed with the personal statement the gospel with which I have been entrusted. This idea is now developed. Paul was not merely commissioned to preach the gospel, but was the living evidence of its meaning and power, and what it had done for him it would do for all men. The passage might seem to be a digression, but is integral to the purpose of the three Epistles, and explains why they are written in the name of Paul. He is taken as the grand exponent of the Christian tradition, alike in his teaching and in his life. The task of the Church is to build itself on the foundation which had been laid by Paul.

12   It was customary in ancient letters to follow the opening salutation with a few words of pious thanks for benefits granted to the writer or to the friend addressed. Paul adopts this custom in his letters, although in every case he fills out the conventional formulae with Christian ideas. Here he gives thanks to Christ 'who put strength into me.' The reference is to his conversion, which at the same time was his call to be an apostle. In receiving the task he had also received strength to perform it. The call had not been fortuitous, though it came to one so unlikely as Paul. In appointing him to apostolic service Christ had judged him to be **trustworthy**, although he had formerly shown himself to be **a blasphemer and a persecutor and a wanton aggressor**. The words are so chosen as to combine the idea of injury to the Church with that of defiance of Christ Himself. Christ had called one who seemed to be His open enemy, perceiving, under all appearances, one

13   whom He could trust. **I obtained mercy because in my unbelief I acted** ignorantly. The sentiment is that of Luke xxiii. 34 (' forgive them ; for they know not what they do '), but no parallel need be sought for. Ignorance has always been regarded as the best excuse for error. It must be noted that in the present verse unbelief is the result, not the cause, of

ignorance. Christ had perceived that Paul was an unbeliever
because he was ignorant, and therefore pitied instead of condemning him. Ignorance which was caused by unbelief would
have been no ground for mercy. A contradiction has sometimes been found between this verse and 2 Tim. i. 3, where Paul
declares that he, like his forefathers, had always served God
with a pure conscience. But the two statements are quite
consistent. Paul's conscience was pure when he rejected the
gospel, for his unbelief was entirely due to ignorance. He
had been chosen precisely because Christ saw in him, unbeliever as he was, a sincere and therefore trustworthy man.
All that he needed was **the grace of our Lord,** which was now 14
given to him in overflowing measure, and along with it **the
faith and love that Christ Jesus** inspires (literally, ' in Christ
Jesus '—i.e. imparted through a living relation to Christ).
Paul himself would not thus have described faith and love as
separate from grace, and given in addition to it. He thought
of the Divine grace as involving everything ; it kindles the
response of faith, and the faith expresses itself in love.

We now meet for the first time with the formula ' sure is the 15
word,' which occurs a number of times in the Pastoral Epistles.
It is evidently meant to mark a quotation, and there have
been various guesses as to the source which is quoted. From
the nature of the ' sure words,' it must have been a Christian
source, and one so familiar that the readers would at once
recognize it. Moreover it must have been known in the
Church for some time, or these quotations from it could not
have been put into the mouth of Paul. Most of the ' sayings '
have a rhythmical character, so marked that it adheres to
them even in the English translation. They are probably
taken from some early liturgy, or from hymns in which the
Christian confession was embodied. From the first the
worship of the Church was enthusiastic, and gave rise spontaneously to lyrical utterance. We learn from Paul that at
every meeting there was someone to whom the Spirit would
suggest a song (1 Cor. xiv. 26), and the brethren are admonished, in another Epistle, to ' admonish one another with
psalms and hymns and spiritual songs ' (Col. iii. 10). Most of

these outbursts would be crude and ephemeral, like those which have always come into being, almost of their own accord, at religious revivals. Now and then, however, something would be thrown out in the heat of the moment which had real poetical value, and which was treasured and often repeated. The New Testament writings contain a number of lyrical passages which seem to have been originally Christian hymns—e.g. the songs in the first two chapters of Luke, in the book of Revelation, in Eph. v. 14. To these may be added the 'faithful' or 'sure words' of the Pastoral Epistles. Sometimes the phrase introduces the saying quoted, and sometimes follows it. Here it plainly refers to the saying that comes after, **and which is described not only as ' sure ' (in the sense of ' trustworthy '), but as ' worthy of all acceptance '—i.e. of the heartiest welcome, deserving all praise, Christ Jesus came into the world to save sinners.** The phrase ' came into the world ' is repeatedly used in the Gospel and First Epistle of John. That it should also occur here may be only a matter of accident, but possibly the hymn quoted had its origin in the circle that produced the Johannine writings. **Of the sinners whom it was the work of Christ to save, I am foremost.** In 1 Cor. xv. 9 Paul also says that he, who had once persecuted the Church, is ' the least of the apostles ' ; and in a similar mood he calls himself (Eph. iii. 8) ' less than the least of all saints.' In the present verse, however, we cannot but feel that the self-abasement is morbid and unreal ; it suggests a type of piety which is out of keeping with the manly sincerity of Paul. The greatness of his sin is made the very ground of his conver-

16 sion. Since he was the very worst of men, he was selected to be a crowning example of what Christ might do by His power and mercy. This is expressed by saying that Paul was meant to serve as a **typical illustration**, or, to take the word in its literal meaning, an ' outline.' Before attempting his final work, an artist or author prepares a sketch in which he tries to indicate his main idea. So Christ, the great artist of noble lives, had used Paul for His experiment ; by His mercy to this wicked man He showed what might be made of unpromising material. **As they thought of Paul, all who were to believe**

could place full confidence in Christ. The word ' believe ' is here used with a prefix which implies the resting of a weight on a sure basis. Men are to rely on Christ not only for their life in the present, but for life in eternity. This is one of the dominant thoughts of the Pastorals, and is emphasized by the 17 doxology which follows. As he thinks of the eternal life which is given through Christ, the writer praises God who reigns eternally. The title ' King of the ages ' (King of eternity) is found in the apocryphal writings, and was probably used in Jewish prayers. It ultimately goes back to the Babylonian idea of world periods or millennial cycles, which in the heavenly order correspond to our earthly years. Through them all God remains sovereign. The conception of God as invisible and dwelling alone is also Jewish, while the epithet ' incorruptible ' or immortal betrays a Greek philosophical influence ; God is outside of the material sphere—pure being as opposed to the process of change and becoming. This Greek conception is peculiarly prominent in Johannine thought, although it pervades the whole of the later New Testament. Doxologies similar to this one are characteristic of Paul's Epistles (cf. Gal. i. 5 ; Rom. xi. 36 ; Phil. iv. 20). With the Jews, as with Mohammedans to-day, it was customary to add some expression of praise and reverence after uttering the name of God. Paul turns these conventional forms into true prayers. Thinking of God his heart is filled with thanksgiving for God's mercy to men.

THE CHARGE TO TIMOTHY (i. 18–20)

I transmit these injunctions to you, Timotheus my son, in 18
    accordance with what the prophets said who first directed
    me to you ; fight the good fight on these lines, holding 19
    to faith and a good conscience. Certain individuals have
    scouted the good conscience and thus come to grief over 20
    their faith—including Hymenaeus and Alexander, whom
    I have made over to Satan. That will teach them to stop
    their blasphemous ongoings !

After the long digression the writer now prepares to take up

the subject of his letter, which has been left hanging in the air
18 since verse 3. First, however, he feels it necessary to state
why Timothy is the fit recipient of the charge now laid on him.
' I transmit this counsel to you, Timotheus my son, in accordance with the prophecies which led forward to you.' Occasion
is here taken to introduce one of the underlying ideas of the
two letters to Timothy. Paul, who is nearing the end of his
career, leaves his work as a trust or deposit with the man
designated to be his successor. The duty of Timothy is to
keep inviolate what is thus committed to him. Timothy is no
doubt to be taken as representative of all later Church leaders.
They stand in the place which Paul once occupied, and are to
guard the message as it has come from his hands.

As Paul's spiritual son, Timothy is his heir; but he also holds
this place in virtue of certain prophecies which had preceded
Paul's choice of him. The reference, as is evident from a later
passage (iv. 14), is to Christian prophecy. No important step was
taken in the Early Church until the sanction of the Spirit had
been obtained through the utterance of prophets (a very notable
instance is the appointment of Saul and Barnabas in Acts
xiii. 1, 2). With regard to Timothy a number of emphatic
prophecies had been made, either at Lystra, where he was
received into the Church, or at some later time when he was
promoted to be a colleague of Paul. These prophecies are
vividly described as ' going on before towards you '—i.e. while
he was still obscure they had singled him out as a coming
man. He is now reminded of this, at once to impress on him
his solemn obligations, and to assure him that Divine help will
be granted him : on these lines (lit. ' in them '—in the confidence inspired by these prophecies) fight the good fight. This
metaphor, which meets us several times in the Epistles (1 Tim.
vi. 12 ; 2 Tim. iv. 7), was a favourite one among Christians
almost from the first. Fidelity to the gospel in those early
days involved a warfare, almost in a literal sense. Not only
was the world hostile, but it was believed that invisible powers
of evil (' spiritual wickedness in high places ') had conspired
against the cause of Christ. In the well-known passage of
Ephesians just quoted (Eph. vi. 2–7) the Christian is described

16

as a soldier in full armour, battling with these deadly enemies ; and all through the first three centuries we find the term ' soldier of Christ ' used almost as another name for Christian. The fight is called good or ' noble ' inasmuch as it aims at the highest of all victories, and is free from sordid methods and selfish ends. Nothing is said in detail, as in the Ephesian passage, of the equipment of the Christian soldier. It is 19 enough that he should keep hold of faith and a good conscience. Both are necessary, for some have come to grief by making light of the demands of conscience ; their practice has been at variance with their faith, and the result has been that their faith also has suffered shipwreck. It may be that like other controversialists the writer is unjust to his opponents, attributing their wrong opinions to moral defects. Yet the main idea is true and penetrating. More often than we know, religious error has its roots in moral rather than in intellectual causes. Examples are given of two men, Hymenaeus and Alexander, 20 whose faith has thus been ruined. Hymenaeus is mentioned again in 2 Tim. ii. 17, and Alexander is possibly the same as the ' smith ' of 2 Tim. iv. 16 ; he may also be the Alexander of Acts xix. 23, who plays a somewhat dubious part in the riot incited by Demetrius at Ephesus. He seems to figure in the account of the riot as a Jew who had attached himself to Paul and had then joined with his countrymen in opposing him. According to the passage before us, Paul had taken the severest measures with these two men, and made them over to Satan. The meaning is no doubt the same as in 1 Cor. v. 3, where the incestuous man is ' delivered to Satan '—i.e. excommunicated. The Church was regarded as a sanctuary from Satan's power, and those expelled from it were thereby given back to Satan, who would now treat them as captured deserters. It was firmly believed in the Early Church that persons thrown out from its communion were exposed to terrible dangers, not only moral but physical. In some cases the apprehension of such danger would doubtless result in bodily sickness and even death. In the Epistle to Titus (iii. 10, 11) a more lenient treatment of false teachers seems to be contemplated ; they are not to suffer punishment, but to be reasoned with gently as erring brothers. But in the present passage the offenders are made over to Satan with a view to their final rescue. By the troubles which will overtake them they are to 'learn not to blaspheme.' The method employed with heretics is still one of persuasion, although it is recognized that in some instances the offender must be disciplined before he will return to a better mind.

DIRECTIONS FOR PUBLIC WORSHIP (ii. 1–7)

ii.

1 Well, my very first counsel is that supplications, prayers, petitions, and thanksgiving, are to be offered for all men—

2 for kings and all in authority, that we may lead a quiet,

3 tranquil life in all godliness and gravity. It is good to pray

4 thus, it is acceptable to our Saviour, to the God who desires all men to be saved and to attain the knowledge of

5 the truth. For ' there is one God ' and ' one intermediary

6 between God and men, the man Christ Jesus who gave Himself as a ransom for all ':—in due time this was

7 attested, and I am appointed to be its herald and apostle (I am not telling a lie, it is the truth), to teach the Gentiles faith and truth.

The theme which was interrupted in i. 3 is now resumed. Paul has some further injunctions to lay on Timothy, in addition to those he had given at Ephesus. In the first place he deals with Church regulations, and this section (ii. 1–iii. 16) falls into two parts : (1) arrangements for worship and behaviour (ii. 1–15) ; (2) the appointment of officers (iii. 1–13). The whole section is rounded off with a ' sure word,' part of a hymn in praise of Christ.

1 These directions for the communal life begin naturally with the matter of public worship, and the opportunity is taken to indicate the Christian attitude to the State. It was commonly believed among pagans that the Church was a secret society, aiming at sinister political ends. In order to allay such suspicions the writer advises that prayer should be made for the Government. This was no mere gesture, to conciliate

18

the ruling powers, but the expression of a real element in the Christian religion. Christ had come for all men, and in their service of Him Christians were to feel themselves united with the whole society in which they lived and to pray for those who looked after its welfare.

The **very first counsel**, therefore, is concerned with public prayer ; the Church exists above all else for worship, and everything in its life depends on the right ordering of its worship. To emphasize the importance of common prayer, it is described by four different words which are practically synonymous. The writer may wish to suggest that a number of elements must enter into a complete prayer, but his chief purpose is simply to make it clear that prayer is the cardinal act of worship : everything in the service is prayer, in varying form. It is remarkable that nothing is said of the sacraments or the exercise of spiritual gifts, which are so fully discussed in First Corinthians. The reason may be that interest is centred, throughout the Pastorals, on the practical life of the Church. Worship is considered not so much from a purely religious point of view as in its bearing on Christian activity. Even when he speaks of prayer the writer does not think of the soul's communion with God, but of prayer on behalf of others —**for all men, and particularly for kings and all in authority.** 2 From the mention of ' kings,' in the plural, it has been inferred that the Epistle was written in the time of Hadrian or the Antonines, when a colleague was associated with the reigning emperor. The plural, however, is more likely meant to give comprehensiveness. Local rulers are to be prayed for as well as the emperor ; and the ordinance is to hold good for future times and under all forms of government. From a very early time the Church followed the practice of offering public prayer for the head of the State, and a liturgical prayer of this kind is contained in the First Epistle of Clement, which is probably earlier in date than the Pastorals. The practice may have been taken over from the synagogue, which was allowed to use prayer for the emperor as a substitute for worshipping him as a divinity. Even without this precedent the Church would be led by its own principles, as this passage suggests, to make prayer for those **in authority.** Conscious of a duty to all men, it would remember before God those in whom the whole community was represented. Nothing is said as to the nature of this prayer for rulers, and the words that follow do not state the petitions, but only the reason for making them, **that we may lead a tranquil life.** This has sometimes been taken to mean ' that we may be left alone '—i.e. that by professing loyalty we may deprive the heathen Government of all pretext for persecution. But the writer may fairly be acquitted of this time-serving motive. All through the passage he is manifestly thinking of the large outlook which belongs to the very nature of the gospel. Christians are to think of themselves as bound up with all mankind, and are to seek their own well-being in that of their fellow-men. In praying that God may direct their rulers they will promote the general peace, and thereby their own. At the same time they desire full opportunity to practise their religion. For other men a well-ordered government is the necessary condition for worldly comfort : Christians require it that they may live in all godliness **and gravity.** The word ' godliness ' (as has been noted in the Introduction) is practically equivalent in these Epistles to ' religion ' ; and ' gravity ' is the visible expression of the religious frame of mind. The desire of the Christian is to keep true to his religion in all his conduct, and even in his appearance and demeanour. For this purpose he needs the ordered life which is only possible under a wise and peaceful government.

3 · At this point the practical directions seem to be interrupted by a purely theological passage. It is not, however, a digression. The demand for prayer **for all men** calls naturally for an explanation, and this is found in the Christian conception of God. **It is good to pray thus, it is acceptable to God our Saviour.** A point is brought out in this translation which is overlooked in the older version. **Good** and **acceptable** have not to be taken together. The thought is rather that largeness of sympathy is right and ennobling ; everyone feels instinctively

4 that this is so. But it is also agreeable to God, for, while He is the Saviour of us Christians, **He desires all men to be saved ;** what He has done for us, He is seeking to do for all men, and

they can only be saved, as we have been, by attaining to right knowledge. Several times in these Epistles the Christian message is described as the **Truth,** and a similar usage is characteristic of the Fourth Gospel. In John, however, the idea is suggested that Christ is the manifestation of ultimate reality ; in the Pastorals little more is implied than that Christianity is the true religion, now offered to all. The reason why it is so offered is set forth in the next words. **There is one 5 God** was the fundamental tenet of Judaism, and was expressed in the great verse of Deuteronomy which was repeated at every religious service, ' Hear, O Israel, the Lord our God is one God.' This belief was combined in Judaism with religious exclusiveness, but Paul had shown that it logically involved his world-wide mission. ' Is He the God of the Jews only ? Nay, also of the Gentiles, if indeed God is one ' (Rom. iii. 29). This Pauline thought is elaborated in the present passage. God must intend His message for all men since He is one ; and it is added that His Mediator also is one. Moffatt may be right in regarding this second part of the sentence as quoted from a Church confession, but it is more probably the writer's own comment on the familiar words of scripture. The conception of Christ as the Mediator, the great High-priest through whom we have access to God since He shares in the attributes both of God and man, is the main theme of the Epistle to the Hebrews. It is possible that the writer was acquainted with Hebrews, and when he says that Christ gave **Himself as a ransom for all 6** he may be echoing the thought of that Epistle that Christ made a sacrifice in which He was Himself both priest and victim (Heb. ix. 11–15). More likely the name ' Mediator ' as 5 applied to Christ was current in the Church, and was used independently by the authors of Hebrews and the Pastorals. Perhaps it is here employed with a side-reference to gnostic theories which had become prevalent. For gnosticism the ' Mediator ' or intermediary was a heavenly being who had casually united Himself with the man Jesus, and separated from Him on the eve of the Crucifixion. In the heathen cults which underlay gnosticism the agent of redemption was always a divinity, who could have no real connexion with this lower world. A protest against such theories may be implicit in the emphatic reference to the man Christ Jesus. If Christ is really to mediate between God and man He must Himself have lived a fully human life. The double name Christ Jesus has a pregnant significance if the verse is understood against the background of gnostic heresy. There was not a heavenly Christ, different from a man Jesus whom He used as His instrument, but one indissoluble personality, and it was that of a man, who was at once Christ and Jesus. It is to be noted that Christ is now dissociated from all ideas of nationality and earthly circumstance. He stands out simply as ' man,' representative of all men and Mediator for all. The description of Him as a ransom connects itself not so much with the priestly ideas of Hebrews as with the saying in Mark x. 45, ' to give Himself a ransom for many.' There is no indication of how the ' ransom ' is to be understood. The writer is interested, not in some given doctrine of atonement, but in the one fact that Christ died for all men. For this reason he uses a compound word (' vicarious ransom ') to bring out more pointedly the thought that Christ surrendered Himself (we need not ask why or to whom) in place of all mankind.

There has always been difficulty as to the exact meaning and sequence of the next words, which are literally to be translated ' the testimony at his own time.' Changes are made in some of the manuscripts to straighten out the grammar and sense ; but, while the sentence is awkwardly expressed, its general meaning seems to be clear, and is well brought out in our rendering. The act by which Christ gave Himself as a ransom was the testimony of God's love to all men and His desire to save them ; and it came in the time appointed. According to another view, there is an abrupt transition from the saving act itself to the witness now borne to it by the apostles ; ' Christ gave Himself, and this is the substance of the message which is now being proclaimed.' This meaning, however, can hardly be extracted from the text, and in the words that follow a distinction is made between the apostolic witness and God's 7 own ' testimony ' : ' to which '—i.e. to the truth attested by God—I was appointed herald and apostle. Paul's part had been simply to make known the truth which had been given through Christ. It could be said of him, as of John the Baptist in the Fourth Gospel, that he was not that light, but was sent to bear witness of that light. At the same time he never doubted that he had a real commission to that office. His claim to be an apostle had been fiercely called in question, and the whole Epistle to the Galatians was written in order to vindicate it. In the light of that Epistle we must explain the parenthesis, **I am not telling a lie, it is the truth.** This has sometimes been regarded as a mere borrowed phrase (cf. Rom. ix. 1 ; 2 Cor. xi. 31 ; Gal. i. 25) which is here thrown in irrelevantly. Whether borrowed or not, the strong assertion of veracity is quite in place. Not only is Paul a genuine apostle, but he has been called **to teach the Gentiles faith and truth** (or perhaps better 'in faith and truth'). In 1 Cor. xii. 29 we hear of three orders in the primitive ministry—apostles, prophets, teachers —and it has been suggested that in the present passage Paul claims to unite the three functions in his own person. But at the time when these Epistles were written the three words had lost their technical significance, and we need see nothing here but a strong assertion that Paul was fully accredited to his office of proclaiming the gospel. This task he has discharged ' in faith and truth '—i.e. with entire fidelity.

Behaviour in Public Worship (ii. 8–15)

Now I want the men to offer prayer at any meeting of the 8 church ; and let the hands they lift to heaven be holy— they must be free from anger and dissension. Women in 9 turn are to dress modestly and quietly in seemly garb ; they are not to adorn themselves with plaits of hair, with gold or pearls or expensive finery, but with good deeds (as 10 befits women who make a religious profession). A 11 woman must listen quietly in church and be perfectly submissive ; I allow no woman to teach or dictate to men, 12 she must keep quiet. For Adam was created first, then 13 Eve ; and Adam was not deceived, it was Eve who was 14 deceived and who fell into sin. However, women will get 15

safely through childbirth, if they continue to be faithful
and loving and holy as well as unassuming.

The reference to Paul's commission is meant to give weight
to the instructions which now follow. As one who has been
divinely appointed and who has been faithful to his trust, he
can speak with full authority ; and thus from the general direction that prayer should be made for all men he passes to more
8 definite injunctions on the subject of prayer. **I want the men
to offer prayer at any meeting of the church**—lit. ' in every
place.' The passage opens, like a royal decree, with a wish
that is equivalent to a command. As an apostle Paul can
legislate for the Church, and he can do so without encroaching
on personal liberty since he deals only with public prayer. In
private devotion each man must approach God in his own way,
but in common worship there must be rules to ensure order and
dignity. He addresses himself first to the men, whose place it is
to conduct the public worship. As yet the primitive custom
was still in force that all the men present were permitted, and
indeed were expected, to take some part in the service (cf. 1
Cor. xiv. 26) ; and the instructions given are to be followed
' in every place.' The time was yet distant when there were
regular buildings set apart for Christian use. Meetings were
generally held in the house of some member who could put a
large room at the disposal of the community. Wherever these
meetings were held, the prayer was to be made in one stated
manner. The man who prayed was to stand with uplifted
hands. This was the posture usually adopted in ancient times,
and there are many allusions to it in both the Old and New
Testaments. It is illustrated in the ' Orantes ' of the Catacombs,
which represent a figure with outstretched arms and hands
with the palm raised upward, symbolic of awaiting a gift from
above. Kneeling, in token of submission, was also a Jewish
practice (cf. Ps. xcv. 6 ; Dan. vi. 10 ; Luke xxii. 41 ; Acts ix.
40), and sometimes we hear of prostration (Matt. xxvi. 39,
xvii. 6 ; Rev. xi. 16), as in Mohammedan worship still. In the
present verse a special significance is given to the gesture of the
lifted hands. They are to be held up as if for inspection, to

show that they are holy. As other religions demanded a ritual purity as the condition of approach to God, so Christianity required a moral purity, and this is conceived as evident in the hands with which man performs his work. The hands must be pure, and the heart likewise, from anger and dissension. This latter word may also mean 'doubts'; but from the whole tenor of the passage it has to be taken in a moral and not an intellectual sense. Before asking God for forgiveness we must 'forgive those who trespass against us.'

From the men the writer turns to the women. Their part in 9 the service is a silent one, but they, too, are to have the spirit of prayer, and to show it in their whole demeanour. **Women in turn are to appear in seemly garb.** A word is used which applies not only to dress but to the whole deportment. By her appearance and bearing the woman must show that she is in the right frame of mind; she must conduct herself with modesty and self-control. The word rendered quietly is taken over from Greek ethics, where it denotes one of the four cardinal virtues, along with courage, justice, wisdom; it occurs a number of times in the Pastorals, and here suggests not only the curbing of aimless thoughts, but a mood of reverence. Women are to adorn themselves, therefore, not with outward show, but with good deeds, as befits women who 10 make a religious profession. This might also be rendered 'as becomes women who show their piety through good works,' and the difficulty would thus be avoided that a charitable life cannot be inferred from a devout behaviour in church; the opposite is too often true. But the meaning is that a life of known uprightness and kindness is itself sufficient adornment. For that part, a good life does, in some way, reveal itself in the outward appearance, and it is worth noting that this thought is constantly in the writer's mind. He is anxious that in the Christian man or woman the inward and the outward should go together. There must be dignity in the Christian life as well as spiritual worth.

It has been assumed that a woman's part in public worship 11 should be a silent one, and this requirement is now stated and explained. We have to remember that the writer lived in an ancient society, which was easily shocked by any kind of publicity on the part of women. He was aware, too, that Christian women, with their new sense of emancipation, were often tempted to go too far, and so brought suspicion and disrepute on the Church. It must further be observed that the restrictions which he places on women apply only to their part in public worship. He wishes, as we shall see later, to enlist their active help in the service of the Church, and puts their duties on the same footing as those of men. But from a sense of decorum, or an old-fashioned prejudice, he is unwilling that they should make themselves too conspicuous in public.

A woman must listen quietly, with all submission. Perhaps there is a suggestion here that sometimes she may learn very little from the masculine wisdom, and may feel inclined to question it. Even then she must repress herself and be silent.

12 **I allow no woman to teach or dictate to men.** The rule is laid down authoritatively in the name of the great apostle, but it is doubtful whether Paul would have expressed himself quite so strongly. He was indeed averse to women making themselves heard in the assembly (1 Cor. xiv. 35), but he by no means forbade them to teach. Priscilla was one of the most valued of his colleagues, and was the teacher of the learned and eloquent Apollos. Euodias and Syntychê are commended as ' women who toiled with me in the message ' (Phil. iv. 3). Although women are forbidden in 1 Corinthians to put themselves forward at the public meeting, it is assumed that they take their part with the men in praying and prophesying (1 Cor. xi. 5). Perhaps in the present passage the word **teach** is to be taken in the technical sense of making a set public address. The reference to ' dictating ' or ' domineering ' has also to be understood in its context. Women are to keep silent in the meeting and not to pose as men's superiors by laying down the law to them.

13 A curious passage follows in which the restriction on women is defended from scripture. **For Adam was created first, then**
14 **Eve ; and it was Eve who was deceived and fell into sin.** Two reasons for the subordination of women are found in the story of Genesis. On the one hand, Eve was created after Adam,

showing that her place was secondary. On the other hand, it was she who yielded to the voice of the serpent. In Rom. v. 12 Paul also alludes to the temptation in Eden, but he grants that it was Adam who fell, and does not mention Eve. The passage before us does not contradict that in Romans, for it only points out that Adam was not directly deceived, but followed the example of Eve. It might be argued that this puts Adam into a still worse position, since he was guilty of weakness as well as disobedience. But the exposition is based, after the rabbinical manner, not so much on the facts as on the literal words by which they are recorded in scripture. The woman said, ' The serpent deceived me ' (Gen. iii. 13), while the man did not make this confession. Thus the woman admitted herself to be the transgressor, and in this state of sin she has remained. It has to be remembered that in the ancient mind a peculiar significance attached to the story in Genesis, which was accepted as strict history and was supposed to pre-figure the whole destiny of the human race in the persons of its first progenitors. Adam and Eve were not only two individuals, but man and woman as they were henceforth to be. In every problem concerning the relation of the sexes guidance was sought in the archetypal story, with results that now strike us as childish and unnatural. It must also be remembered that the writer is here discussing not the large question of the position of woman, but the definite one as to whether women should act as teachers. He may well have thought that the Bible story had a real relevance to this question. The first woman was easily deceived, and all women since are liable to be misled by plausible appearances or by whim and fancy. It might therefore be wise to debar them from public teaching.

The allusion to the story in Genesis has possibly to be carried 15 over into the difficult verse which follows. According to the view adopted by Moffatt, the reference is to the penalty imposed on the woman in Gen. iii. 16. Although she must submit to this penalty and bear children with danger, **women will yet come through it safely, if they continue** in faith and love and consecration, along with self-control. But the Greek is hardly capable of any other translation than ' she will be saved through childbirth ' ; and this idea, absurd on the face of it, becomes more so when it is added that all the Christian virtues are necessary besides. Faith and love and a holy life are apparently worthless unless a woman happens also to be a mother. No Christian community, with the possible exception of the early Mormons, has ever held this preposterous doctrine, and it does not become much more feasible when ' child-bearing ' is taken to imply the nurture of children rather than the bare fact of maternity. For that part, in this very Epistle (v. 5f.), it is enjoined that special care and honour should be bestowed on Christian widows who have no children to provide for them ; such women, free from all household duties, are to be employed in preference to others for pious duties, and they are certainly not supposed to have no part in salvation because they are childless. According to one view the present verse has reference to the promise made to Eve that her seed will crush the serpent's head (Gen. iii. 15). This was taken by the Early Church as a prophecy of the Messiah ; and the curse pro-nounced on Eve was thus conjoined with a promise of salva-tion. But even granting that the writer understood the verse in this manner, he cannot have found in it a promise that Eve herself would be saved, and this is the point required. It seems best to take the Greek preposition in the phrase ' through childbearing,' not in its usual sense of ' by means of ' but as denoting a condition. ' She will be saved even though she must bear children.' That is, Eve, the representative woman, was condemned to painful child-birth as the penalty for her sin, and this penalty is still exacted. But woman, no less than man, will be saved, in spite of the continuing mark of Divine dis-pleasure, if women live the true Christian life. The writer, in fact, is making a sort of apology for what he has said about women. He has implied that in consequence of Eve's trangres-sion they are permanently under a cloud ; but he adds, ' do not mistake me ; though still reminded of their sin they fully share in the offered salvation.' The writer's mind passes from women in general as typified in Eve to particular women who fulfil the Christian requirements of faith, love, and holy living, combined with self-control. This last virtue is not a specifically Christian one, and perhaps is added to link up the digression with the main theme of the passage. Women are not to teach in public, but to observe the decorum which the world expects of them. In their piety they must not forget the exercise of this restraint.

THE QUALIFICATIONS OF A BISHOP (iii. 1-7)

iii.

It is a popular[1] saying that 'whoever aspires to office is set 1 upon an excellent occupation.' Well, for the office of a 2 bishop a man must be above reproach ; he must be married only once, he must be temperate, master of himself, unruffled, hospitable, a skilled teacher, not a drunkard, not 3 violent but lenient and conciliatory, not a lover of money, able to manage his own household properly and to keep his 4 children submissive and perfectly respectful (if a man does 5 not know how to manage his own household, how is he to look after the church of God ?) ; he must not be a new 6 convert, in case he gets conceited and incurs the doom passed on the devil ; also, he must have a good reputation 7 among outsiders, in case he incurs slander and is trapped by the devil.

A transition is now made from the worship to the ministry of the Church, and the section opens with another of the quoted sayings. Many expositors, both ancient and modern, 1 would place the formula, ' It is a sure word,' at the end of the previous chapter ; but there is nothing in the pedantic allegory of the trespass of Eve which can ever have passed from mouth to mouth as a watchword of Christian wisdom. The natural reference is to the opening verse of the new chapter, but the difficulty is that there is nothing in the verse that seems to have religious value. In some manuscripts the formula runs, It is a popular saying, and this reading is preferred by Moffatt. But the mass of textual evidence is against it, and it has all

---

1 Reading ἀνθρώπινος. It is more easy to understand how it was altered to πιστός for the sake of uniformity with i. 15, etc., than vice versa.

the appearance of being substituted by some early editor who assumed, from the other instances in the Epistles, that the formula, ' It is a faithful saying,' must have a direct religious reference. In itself, however, the formula means nothing more than that the saying in question may be relied on, whatever may be its nature. The ' saying ' which is quoted here may have been a current proverb, or perhaps the familiar opening of the charge given at an ordination. At the same time there must have been something in the saying that lent it a pungent quality. This may have consisted in attaching a lofty sense to two Greek words that commonly bore a low one (' It is a noble glutton that is greedy for Church office '). Wherever he found it, the writer quotes the saying by way of graceful suggestion that only good men will seek to be bishops. He wants the Church, however, to make sure that none but 2 good men will be appointed. **For the office of a bishop a man must be above reproach ;** not only must his past life be free from blame, but there must be nothing in his habits or character which can give offence. The Greek reads simply ' the bishop must be above reproach,' and from this it has sometimes been inferred that the system had now arisen under which a single bishop was in charge of each community. But there is nothing else, either in this Epistle or in the two others, to warrant such a conclusion. All that is meant is ' the typical bishop '—just as we speak of ' the soldier,' ' the physician.' It can hardly be doubted that the term ' bishop ' in these Epistles is synonymous with ' presbyter ' or ' elder.' This would seem to be apparent from a passage in Titus (i. 5–9) which is closely parallel to this one, and which uses the terms ' bishop ' and ' elder ' as interchangeable. That there were a number of these officers in each Church, is repeatedly made clear. They formed a group or board, known as the ' presbyterate,' which acted together in solemn functions like that of ordination (1 Tim. iv. 14). The word ' bishop ' (from the Greek *episkopos*) means literally ' an overseer,' and was used in the pagan world to denote a governing man in any civic or religious organization. Among the Jews the leading men of the synagogue were known as the presbyters or ' elders,' and the name was taken over, as we learn from the book of Acts, by the Primitive Church in Jerusalem. Apparently there was a period when the Jewish and Gentile terms were used concurrently ; but as the Church became more fully organized the bishops were separated from the elders, or rather one man was made president of the group of elders, and the name of ' bishop,' along with the full power of oversight, was reserved for him. At a still later stage the bishop became the head, not merely of a single community, but of a whole district, i.e. a ' diocese ' made up of a cluster of separate Churches. It is one of the chief evidences of the early date of the Pastorals that the one-man episcopate has not yet arisen. When Ignatius wrote his letters (about A.D. 116) the new system had been generally adopted, at least in the Eastern Churches, but there is no suggestion of it in the Pastorals. Thus while the organization has developed beyond that of the apostolic age it still bears the primitive mark.

This inference is confirmed by the account given in this passage of the bishop's qualifications. They are all of a general nature, affecting character rather than professional fitness. A bishop must be ' husband of one wife.' This has sometimes been taken to imply that only married men were eligible, but a rule of this kind would be contrary to the whole tenor of the passage, which deals with character rather than status. Neither can it be polygamy which is forbidden, for this was never practised in the civilized regions of Asia Minor. Perhaps Moffatt is right in translating **he must be married only once** ; later in the Epistle widows who do not re-marry are singled out as worthy of honour, and this ideal of a single marriage might hold good for men also who aspired to high office in the Church. But perhaps the meaning simply is that a bishop must show an example of strict morality. As a man of mature years he would presumably be married, and in the married relation, above all others, he must be **above reproach.** He must further be **temperate** in the wider sense of the term **(master of himself)**—since drunkenness is expressly forbidden a little later. He must be prudent and dignified, **hospitable** and able to teach. This probably does not refer to official teaching, for in v. 17 the elders who devote themselves to this

work are singled out from the others. The ' teaching ' of which
every bishop must be capable is the giving of good counsel.
He must be an approachable man, who can deal wisely and
3 sympathetically with all who need advice. The directions
proceed that he must not be a drunkard or violent, but lenient
and conciliatory, not a lover of money. It is to be noted that
the idea throughout is that of moderation. Excess in wine or
anger or covetousness is forbidden, but no demand is made for
saint-like self-denial. The writer never forgets that the Church
is made up of ordinary men, and that he must be content with
the best he can get. In the requirement ' not a money-lover '
some would find a suggestion that part of a bishop's duty was
to administer the Church funds, but this is quite arbitrary ;
the character described is simply that of a wise, well-balanced,
trustworthy man. It is only towards the end that some
account is taken of official fitness, and even then the demands
4 are not specific. The man chosen must be able to manage his
own household properly (including all his dependants and his
private affairs and belongings), and to keep his children submissive and perfectly respectful. The sentence is worded very carefully, to make clear that it is not a stern disciplinarian who is
thought of, but a man whose character has impressed his
5 children, so that they naturally look up to him. This attitude
of a man's own family is accepted as the surest test of his
ability to direct the church, which is like a larger family committed by God, who is its head, to the care of the elders.
6 Again, the bishop must not be a new convert. This word
' neophyte ' means literally ' newly planted,' and seems to
have been used in a technical sense almost from the first.
Perhaps it goes back to Jesus' own parable of the Sower, or
to Paul's comparison of himself to a gardener, who has planted
what his successor waters (1 Cor. iii. 6–9). We have here an
unguarded admission that the Pastorals are considerably later
than the time of Paul. He was the founder of the Church at
Ephesus, and all its members were in his day ' new converts ' ;
though it is of course conceivable that in so young a Church
(just as in a school or college) those of a year or two's standing would count as seniors. In case he gets conceited (lit.

'wrapt in smoke'—lost in a fog of vanity because of his rapid promotion) **and incurs the doom passed on the devil** (lit. 'falls into the judgment of the devil'). Some would here take the word for 'devil' in its original sense of 'accuser' or 'slanderer'; the meaning would thus be that the new convert, thrust into office without due preparation, will do foolish things out of vanity, and so expose himself to malicious gossip. But in the very next verse the word is apparently used for 'devil'; it certainly has this meaning in 2 Tim. ii. 26, and we must give it the same sense here. Some would therefore take the verse as implying that the hostile criticism which the neophyte will draw on himself is inspired by the devil. By his foolish acts he allows the devil to condemn him by the mouths of fault-finders. To this it may be objected that a conceited fool is a air mark for criticism; those who judge him as he deserves will be regarded by none but himself as mouthpieces of the devil. A much more likely interpretation is that adopted by Moffatt. For the sin of pride the devil was condemned, and a vain man lays himself open to the same doom. This gives a simple and quite satisfactory meaning to the difficult phrase; yet perhaps in view of the verse that follows it is best taken as 'a judgment wrought by the devil.' A man who is at the mercy of his own vanity is easily led into many temptations; the devil will soon lure him into some sin for which he will be condemned. So the elder chosen must not only be a mature Christian, but **7 must also have a good reputation among outsiders.** A man who is highly respected in his Church often appears in a very different light to his workmen or business associates. Moreover it was necessary in those early years of the Church that the men who represented it should be favourably known among their fellow-citizens. One who had incurred general ill will, however innocently, would bring suspicion and perhaps danger on the Church. This is implied in the words **in case he incurs slander and is trapped by the devil.** It is possible to explain the thought here in a psychological way. A man who knows himself to be disliked finds it difficult to do just the right thing; he is tempted either to win over his enemies by wrong methods, or to defy them by going too far in the old direction. The man who stands well with his community has nothing to think of but his own conscience. But the writer may have his mind not so much on the elder himself as on the Church which he represents. If he is unpopular with his heathen neighbours, they will put the worst colour on everything he does. He will make some slip, which would be overlooked in another man, and this will be used as a pretext for distressing the Church. The devil is always laying traps for the cause of Christ, and a man who is already disliked will prove the easiest victim.

THE CHOICE OF DEACONS (iii. 8–13)

8 Deacons in turn are to be serious men ; they are not to be tale-
9 bearers nor addicted to drink or pilfering ; they must maintain the divine truth of the faith with a pure con-
10 science. They too must be put on probation ; after that, if they are above reproach, they may serve as deacons.
11 Their wives must be serious too ; they must not be slanderers, they must be temperate and absolutely trust-
12 worthy. Deacons are only to be married once, and they must manage their children and their households properly.
13 For those who do good service as deacons win a good position for themselves as well as great freedom in the faith of Christ Jesus.

8 The word ' deacon ' means literally an ' assistant,' and was used in the first instance to describe the men who helped the fully accredited missionaries. Paul and Barnabas took Mark with them as their ' deacon ' (Acts xiii. 5), partly to attend on them personally, and partly to assist them in the forming of Churches. At an early time it was found convenient to provide the ' elders ' or governing body in each community with a group of subordinates who relieved them of duties which belonged to the practical more than the spiritual side of their work. When Paul wrote to the Philippians he addressed the ' bishops and deacons ' (Phil. i. 1), including the deacons, most probably, because he was to acknowledge a gift of money

which they had taken part in raising. The rules concerning deacons in the present passage are similar to those already laid down for bishops. In both cases the aim is to secure men of sterling character for office in the Church ; but it is noticeable that emphasis is now placed on business qualities as well as on moral and religious worth.

Deacons of the Church would usually be its future elders, so they needed to be men of the same type and character. They were to be **serious** men. This word, which has already occurred several times, denotes at once an inward temper and an outward bearing ; you at once recognize the serious man by the very look of him, as one whom you must respect. Along with this weight of character the deacons must have special virtues—**not tale-bearers nor addicted to drink or pilfering.** In the discharge of his duties a deacon had to mix socially with his fellow-members, and might easily fall into the habits of gossip and drinking. He might also become too keen on money. A word is used in this connexion which means literally ' making base gains,' and it might apply to men who followed some degrading occupation ; but we have doubtless to understand it in an ethical sense. There may be a hint that some men contrived to make a personal gain out of their management of Church finance, but more likely the meaning is that in getting money for the Church the deacons must not resort to sordid methods, by turning Christian charity into a pure matter of business. Above all, they must be religious **men, maintaining the divine truth (lit. the mystery) of the faith with a pure conscience.** The emphasis falls on this sincerity. Men must be chosen who honestly believe what they profess. Their piety must be no mere mask to give them credit with others, but must be the truth they live by. Paul speaks a number of times of the ' mystery ' involved in the Christian message. He means that beneath each fact and doctrine there is a hidden import, bound up with the ultimate purpose towards which God has been ever working. In the Pastorals this idea of ' mystery ' becomes almost conventional ; it is assumed that although men cannot understand the gospel they must accept it with implicit faith as given by God. **Faith** also has come

35

to have a different meaning from what it had for Paul. Instead of the act of self-surrender whereby we yield ourselves to God's grace, it denotes simply a firm belief. Sometimes, as here, it is little more than another name for the Christian religion.

10 To make sure that the deacons have all the qualities required of them, it is added **they must be put on probation.** We are not to think of them as undergoing some formal test, which would serve little purpose where moral and spiritual fitness was in question. The idea is rather that full enquiries should be made, and that the claims of one man should be carefully weighed against those of another. If **they are above reproach, they may serve as deacons.** Nothing is said as to the manner in which the election is finally made. Did the existing body of deacons co-opt their new members? Was there a show of hands on the part of the whole Church? No rules are laid down, for it is assumed that they are in force already. The Pastorals were evidently not intended to be a manual of Church order; they are concerned not with a system, but with the men who are to operate the system.

11 A verse is interposed, in the passage on deacons, in which women are likewise required to be **serious, temperate, trustworthy.** Standing where it does, the verse cannot apply to women in general. According to one view (adopted by Moffatt), the women in question are the **wives** of the deacons. Since the deacon's duties were largely social, his wife would take some part in them; in any case it would not be fitting that a leader of the Church should have a wife out of sympathy with him, who might injure his usefulness. The directions, however, repeat what has been said about deacons, and seem to refer to women who were engaged in the same kind of work. Elsewhere in the Epistle we hear of female assistants (1 Tim. v. 9ff.), and apparently they are contemplated here. In the time of Paul there were already ' deaconesses ' in the Church, and for one of them Paul wrote a letter of introduction which is included in the Epistle to Romans (ch. xvi.). **It** is probably deaconesses who are

36

intended in this verse, although the rule is so framed as to make it applicable to all female workers.

The subject of deacons is resumed, and the conditions laid 12 down for bishops are repeated in much the same words. Competent discharge of all family duties was required of bishops because it gave proof that they might be entrusted with the larger family of the Church. Deacons had not to bear the same responsibility, and a different reason is given for the importance attached to their conduct. **For those who do 13 good service as deacons win a good position** (lit. ' an honourable degree '). The word used is found nowhere else in the New Testament, and means properly a ' step ' (e.g. of an altar or a platform). From early times it has often been taken to imply that the deacons, while subordinate officers, were in the way of promotion ; out of their number the bishops were chosen, and their office was therefore an important one, which had to be filled with the best possible men. This idea, however, seems foreign to the writer's whole intention. He is not concerned with the relative dignity of Church offices, but with the moral qualities they require. He wishes deacons to value their position, not for the chance of promotion which it offers, but for what it is in itself. One feels that the previous instructions would be made ridiculous if they closed on the note, ' Try to be a good deacon, for you will then be in the running for the next vacancy among the elders.' Moreover the **good position** is conjoined with **great freedom in the faith of Christ.** It has therefore to be interpreted in the sense of moral and religious standing. The deacon may be only a subordinate, but when he has done well he gains a position of real influence, and can speak effectively on every matter which concerns the Church. This is possibly the meaning ; but it seems better to take the words in a yet higher sense. The true reward of a good deacon is that he rises in God's own judgment. He attains to ' boldness ' in his faith, to a full confidence that all he has believed is true. In view of the solemn phrase ' the faith which is in Christ Jesus,' we are almost compelled to find this religious significance in the thought. If he were thinking only of the esteem and influence which a deacon gains in the community, the writer would hardly express himself in such terms, from which he passes immediately to the sublime conclusion of this chapter.

THE PURPOSE OF THE DIRECTIONS (iii. 14–16)

14 Though I hope to come to you before long, I am writing to you
15   in this way, in case I am detained, to let you see how people ought to behave within the household of God, which is the church of the living God, the pillar and bulwark of the
16   Truth. And who does not admit how profound is the divine truth of our religion ?—it is He who was

       ' manifest in the flesh,
       vindicated by the Spirit,
       seen by angels,
       preached among the nations,
       believed on throughout the world,
       taken up to glory.'

The rules prescribed have dealt with practical arrangements, and might seem to have little relation to the higher interests of religion. Yet they must not be neglected. They involve the well-being of the Church, and it is the Church that maintains the gospel and offers it to the world. So in these verses we have the key to the inner meaning of the Pastoral Epistles. The writer is no mere ecclesiastic, more concerned with the mechanism of the Church than with its spiritual life. He insists on right order because he feels it to be necessary to true religion. In the life of the Church, as of the individual, body and soul must work together.

14   At the outset we are again reminded of the purpose of the letter. Paul has left Ephesus, intending shortly to return, but meanwhile writes a number of counsels for Timothy's guidance, in case his return may be delayed. We naturally ask why he did not give his directions before he left. When a business or professional man turns over his work for a short period to a substitute, he carefully explains what must be done If he

writes afterwards, it is because of some emergency which could not be foreseen. But the counsels in 1 Timothy have nothing to do with an unlooked-for situation. They are designed, rather, to meet the permanent requirements of a Christian Church, whether at Ephesus or elsewhere. Paul's fear that he may be **detained** is no adequate reason why a letter of this kind should have been written. So the more we examine it the more we feel that the setting of these Epistles is artificial; they were written in the name of Paul for the purpose of showing **how to behave** (the word is a comprehensive one, meant to cover all the relations of life) **in the household of God.** Again the Church is compared to a family, of which God is the head, and in which every member has his appointed place. All must learn to perform their duty in the Church, for it is **the church of the living God,** the God who truly exists and is the source of all life and reality. He has ordained the Church as **the pillar and bulwark of the Truth,** i.e. of the gospel, in which He has revealed Himself. The word translated **bulwark** means literally ' something to rest on,' and is commonly used for a basis or foundation. How can the Church be regarded as the basis of the gospel ? It has always been felt that the relations of Church and gospel ought to have been expressed in just the other way ; the gospel is the sure foundation on which the Church must be built. In view of this difficulty it is held by some commentators that the verse has been wrongly punctuated, and that the words usually taken to describe the Church ought to be thrown into the next sentence : ' Pillar and basis of truth and admittedly great is the mystery, etc.' This construction is grammatically valid, but so awkward that it cannot well be accepted. To say that the mystery is ' great ' after calling it the very foundation of everything would be nothing but an anticlimax. No one, however, would have found any difficulty in the verse if, instead of describing it as the ' foundation,' the writer had called it the ' citadel ' or (in Moffatt's phrase) **the bulwark of the Truth** ; and this, in effect, is what he says. The word (which commonly means ' ground ' or ' basis ') was sometimes used, like our own word ' support,' for anything that keeps you secure though it may not strictly be underneath you. Thus the idea of the verse is simply that the Church exists in order to maintain the faith and protect it from all danger. The image employed is, indeed, a highly appropriate one, for the pillars and supports of a building are meant to uphold the roof. When foundation and walls have been made secure, pillars are set up that the whole structure may be covered in from rain and storm. This is the function of the Church in Christianity, and there is nothing in the present verse to contradict Paul's statement that ' other foundation can no man lay but that which is laid, even Jesus Christ ' (1 Cor. iii. 11).

For that part, this very statement is reaffirmed in the 16 verse which follows. ' And assuredly ' (lit. **who does not admit ?**—with the added suggestion that what all acknowledge may be taken as true) ' great is the mystery of godliness.' **Godliness**, this characteristic word of the Epistles, has been discussed in the Introduction. It includes both the faith and practice of the Christian life, and Moffatt aptly translates it **our religion.** Here it has a special fitness, since the writer is thinking of the practical rules he has just laid down. They may seem only to affect outward living, but this also is part of ' godliness,' which is bound up, as everyone can see, with tremendous issues. It has its motive and purpose in a ' mystery '—i.e. in the Divine plan which is revealed in the Christian message. What is the nature of this message ? The answer is given in words which are plainly a quotation. They do not connect grammatically with what has gone before, and are thrown in, as one might cite a verse of poetry, to conclude and dignify a passage of argument. From the rhythmical form of the lines it is certain that they are taken from some Christian poem, a hymn or a chanted confession. (A hint of this may be conveyed by the word ' confessedly ' which is used just before.) What is given us is evidently the closing part of this lyrical confession of Christ. **He who was manifested in the flesh.** The pronoun must refer to a subject in a previous verse which has not been quoted. In some early manuscripts the pronoun which thus comes so abruptly was changed into a noun by a slight modification of the letters,

so that it read ' God manifested.' But the context shows that
Christ is the subject. His earthly life is regarded as the revelation in visible form of one who in essence was Divine. **Vindicated in the Spirit.** The word used is familiar in the Pauline
Epistles in the sense of ' justify ' or ' declare righteous,' and
some would find a similar meaning here (**vindicated by the
Spirit**). Christ appeared on earth and was put to death as a
false Messiah ; but the Spirit declared Him to be indeed the
Righteous One. The clause, however, is parallel to the preceding one, and ' in Spirit ' must correspond to ' in flesh ' ; as
Christ was manifested in the earthly sphere He was restored
to His true nature in the sphere of Spirit. Or perhaps the
reference is to that ' Spirit of holiness ' which constituted
His inner personality (Rom. i. 4 ; Heb. ix. 14). He appeared
in the flesh, but was ' declared to be the Son of God with
power, according to the Spirit of holiness, by His rising from
the dead.' Attempts have been made to explain **seen by
angels,** from something in the recorded life—e.g. the baptism,
the temptation, the transfiguration ; but in all these episodes
it was Jesus who saw the angels. According to one far-
fetched conjecture, ' angels ' must be taken in the sense of
' messengers ' ; after the Resurrection Christ appeared to the
apostles, who were thus assured that He was still living. More
probably the clue to the meaning is to be found in such
passages as Eph. iii. 10 ; Phil. ii. 10 ; Heb. i. 6. As Christ is
honoured as Lord on earth, so He receives honour in heaven.
In several Jewish apocalypses the Messiah is described as wor-
shipped by angels, and this idea was elaborated in the Early
Church ; the Christian imagination dwelt on the scene in
heaven when Christ returned after His victory and the angels
thronged out to acclaim Him. One has only to remember the
worship of the Lamb by the angels in our Book of Revelation.
Preached among the nations, believed on throughout the world,
are two clauses in which we do not have simply the same fact
repeated in two different forms. The first clause marks the
beginning, after Jesus' death, of a great mission, when the
message proclaimed in Palestine was carried far and wide to
the Gentiles. The second clause marks the consummation. A

time is to come when all men will accept the message and believe in Christ as their Saviour. It is this same train of thought which leads up to the closing words ' taken up in glory.' This might seem to be only another reference to the Ascension, which has already been celebrated ; and many expositors have remarked that there is no logical order or historical sequence in the hymn. Events in the Saviour's career seem to be thrown together at haphazard, and the return to heaven is brought in a second time, by way of a triumphant close. But the hymn, whatever may be its origin, is a careful composition, in which every word is weighted with meaning. It reminds us of the Apostles' Creed, which likewise has for its theme the life and work of Christ, and so proceeds from ' born of the Virgin Mary ' to the Last Judgment. Here the sequence is carried still further, to the time when Christ shall have judged the world and established His Kingdom. After the harvest is fully gathered in, He will be taken up, not to glory, but ' in ' glory—i.e. He will enter on His eternal Kingdom, with His whole work gloriously accomplished.

From the brief fragment preserved to us, it is hard to determine the structure of the hymn. It falls, according to one view, into two verses or stanzas of three lines each, one on the historical life of Jesus, the other on His continued life as Lord of the Church. It might also be divided into three couplets, the first on the incarnation, the second on the exalted life, the third on the final victory. Both of these schemes are a little artificial, and it is difficult to fit the third and the sixth lines into either of them. Perhaps the best division is into two verses, each consisting of two lines, with a third line added by way of refrain or chorus. The first verse tells of Christ's life on earth, the second of his larger life in the Church ; and each of them closes on a note of triumph.

It is singular that in this confessional hymn nothing is expressly said either of the death or the Resurrection. This is the more remarkable when we think of similar confessions which have come to us from the Early Church—e.g. the Apostles' Creed and the great passage in Philippians (ii. 6–11).

We must remember, however, that nothing is left to us but this fragment which our writer quotes. If the first part of the Philippian passage had been lost, and we had only the verses beginning ' God hath highly exalted him,' we should have found a like difficulty. The hymn before us was most probably constructed on lines similar to those of Paul's great outburst. If the whole of it had been preserved, it would certainly have taken its place among the chief treasures of Christian poetry, and we may be thankful even for the noble fragment. The writer of the Pastorals was not interested, as we are, in the hymn itself. He is speaking of the Church, and he quotes the hymn only in so far as it throws some light on the ' mystery,' the Lordship of Christ on which the Church must build its faith.

Warning Against a False Asceticism (iv. 1–5)

iv.

But in later days, the Spirit distinctly declares, certain people 1
will rebel against the faith ; they will listen to spirits of
error and to doctrines that daemons teach through plausible 2
sophists who are seared in conscience—men who prohibit 3
marriage and insist on abstinence from foods which God
created for believing men, who understand the Truth, to
partake of with thanksgiving. Anything God has created 4
is good, and nothing is to be tabooed—provided it is eaten
with thanksgiving, for then it is consecrated by God's word, 5
by the prayer uttered over it.

In the Pastoral Epistles we have constant allusion to certain forms of error which had found entrance into the Church. They are dealt with in the present chapter more fully than elsewhere, although the account given of them is far from explicit. The writer is much more concerned with the practical effects of the new teaching than with the doctrines. So far as we can gather from his vague indications, it was a mixture of Jewish with gnostic speculation, similar in character to the heresy condemned in the Epistle to the Colossians. In

Colossians, however, Paul strikes at the root of the heresy. He shows that it is fatal to Christian faith because it denies that Christ is himself sufficient for man's salvation. The practices in which it results are denounced, as in the Pastorals, but they are shown to spring inevitably out of the religious error. This later writer lays all stress on the practices ; the effects are judged to be wrong, without any enquiry into their cause.

The first section is devoted to the ascetic tendencies which were a marked feature of the new teaching, and it opens with
1 a brief reference to the teachers themselves. **In later days, the Spirit distinctly declares.** Intimations of the Spirit were often given in riddles, but this one had been made in clear, unmistakable terms. The allusion may be to some well-known oracle which was current in the Church. Christian prophets, under the influence of the Spirit, were continually making forecasts of future events, and an important announcement of this kind would be preserved and circulated. Most likely the prediction which is here in the writer's mind is that attributed to Paul himself in his farewell to the Ephesian elders at Miletus : ' For I know this, that after my departing shall grievous wolves enter in, not sparing the flock ' (Acts xx. 29). In the present passage Paul is assumed to be writing at a time previous to that farewell, but he had already received a clear intimation of what will happen **in later times.** A word is here used which denotes that the ' times ' foreseen will be critical. Rebellion on the part of ' some ' will show that invisible powers of evil are at work, seeking through human agents to wean Christ's people from their allegiance. Perhaps there is a reminiscence of Matt. xxiv. 11, 12, where Jesus declares that ' the love of many will wax cold ' just before the decisive conflict. In these coming days men **will listen to spirits of error and the doctrines of demons,** as in the old tales about travellers led off from the true road ' by calling shapes and beckoning shadows dire.' These deceiving powers are supernatural, in
2 the service of Satan, but they take their dwelling in **plausible sophists,** teachers who wear the mask of a Christianity which pretends to be purer and more earnest than that of the Church. **These mouthpieces of evil spirits are said to be seared in their**

own **conscience.** Two interpretations of this difficult phrase are possible : (1) They have been ' cauterized ' (this is the Greek word employed) so as to lose all feeling of right and wrong. If they deceive others, it is because their own conscience has first become utterly perverted ; (2) They have been branded like slaves or criminals, marked out as belonging to Satan ; if others do not recognize them as doing Satan's work under the guise of sanctity, they are aware, in their own conscience, of the brand. This is probably the true meaning. The whole emphasis is on the idea that these human agents are consciously the agents of a spiritual power behind them. Prompted by Satan **they prohibit marriage and insist on ab-** 3 **stinence from foods which God created.** In the Epistle to the Romans Paul has occasion to deal with a class of Christians who abstained from certain kinds of food, confining themselves, it would appear, to strict vegetarianism (Rom. xiv. 1ff.) ; instead of denouncing these brethren ' whose conscience is tender ' he pleads that they should be treated with sympathy, and declares that the great truths of the gospel have nothing to do with matters of meat and drink. For the present writer the ascetic attitude is due to Satanic influence. He is dealing, however, with a different kind of asceticism from that which is excused by Paul. It had its origin (as we know from gnostic documents) not in ritual scruples or in mistaken theories of self-denial, but in the belief that God had not created the natural world. To abstain from marriage and, as far as possible, from food, was held to be necessary before a man could separate himself from the sphere of matter and rise into that of spirit. It is from this point of view that we must explain the writer's vehemence. Although he speaks of practices which appear in themselves quite innocent, he is aware of their implications. He declares, as against the ascetic teachers, that God created everything, that He meant us to enjoy His earthly gifts, and that we ought to do so **with thanksgiving.** The question at stake is that of our whole conception of God. Are we to think of Him as grudging us our earthly life, or are we to find in it a continual proof of His presence and goodness ? It might seem from the words that follow as if God made good things to be enjoyed only by believing men, who understood the Truth—i.e. Christians. Some have taken the words to mean that believers are set free from dietary restrictions which are still binding on Jews and heathens. According to this view a larger choice of dishes is held out as one of the inducements to exchange a false religion for the true one. It is quite certain that nothing so absurd is intended. The argument is rather that, if God has manifestly offered His earthly gifts for man's enjoyment, we cannot possibly believe that He denies them to Christians, who have understood His mind better than any others. This, however, was implied in that false teaching which made asceticism a higher stage of Christianity.

The idea of the previous verse is now stated more explicitly. **Anything God has created is good, and nothing is to be tabooed.** There is possibly an allusion to the first chapter of Genesis, which tells how God considered everything He had made and declared it good. Or perhaps the meaning is that everything which God bestows must be good, since it comes from Him. A gift, however, loses its value unless it is accepted with gratitude, and we must ourselves supply that condition before 5 even the gifts of God are, in the full sense, good. This is in the writer's mind when he says that the gift must be **consecrated.** To be sure, that which proceeds from God does not require any formal consecration; yet for the man who does not recognize it as God's gift it remains common. When it is ' received with thanks ' to the Giver it becomes sacred, a visible pledge of the love and goodness of God. There is some difficulty in the phrase which Moffatt translates **by the prayer uttered over it,** and which is literally ' through the word of God and prayer.' Some would find a reference to the creative word of God. The food we eat, like all other things, came into being by God's command, and is thereby consecrated : we acknowledge this in the prayer of thanksgiving. But the writer is speaking of man's attitude to God's gifts, which lose their sacredness unless they are received in a thankful spirit. So the reference is probably to the custom, adopted by the Church from Judaism, of using words of scripture in the blessing pronounced before and after a meal. The prayer of gratitude by which the gift was consecrated found expression in God's own words.

TIMOTHY'S ATTITUDE TO FALSE TEACHING (iv. 6-10)

Lay all this before the brotherhood, and you will be an excellent minister of Christ Jesus, brought up on the truths of the faith and on the lessons of the good doctrine you have already followed. Shut your mind against these profane, drivelling myths ; train for the religious life. The training of the body is of some small service, but religion is of service in all directions ; it contains the promise of life both for the present and for the future. It is a sure word, it deserves all praise, that ' we toil and strive[1] because our hope is fixed upon the living God, the Saviour of all men ' —of believers in particular. **6 7 8 9-10**

Instead of denouncing the heresies or seeking to confute them, the writer declares that they are to be met positively. In his own life and teaching Timothy is to hold firmly to the true gospel. He is to avoid all vain speculations and train himself and others in the true gospel ; when the truth is thus displayed, falsehood will lose its attraction. The passage throws an instructive light on the whole aim of the Epistles. Although they are written in opposition to wrong tendencies in the Church, they are not controversial. The presentation is at all points constructive. If the Church is to overcome pagan hostility, it must do so by keeping itself pure and admitting to its leadership only such men as will command respect ; if it is to resist the encroachments of false teaching, it must affirm more strongly than ever the true principles of the gospel.

Lay all this before the brotherhood ; or rather, ' lay it under them.' An expressive word is used which carries with it the idea of putting something beneath the feet. The precepts **6**

---

[1] Reading ἀγωνιζόμεθα. The context requires an aggressive, active verb. The ' sure words ' all have a more or less eschatological outlook.

given in the first part of the chapter are to be like stepping-stones which will enable Timothy's hearers to pass securely over treacherous ground. By so acting **you will be an excellent minister of Christ Jesus.** The same word ' minister ' which is elsewhere used for a deacon is here applied to Christian service in general, just as in 2 Tim. iv. 5 the word ' evangelist,' which had formerly a special meaning, is employed in a broad sense for a Church leader. We are thus reminded that ecclesiastical language was in a fluid condition at the time when these Epistles were written ; particular terms which are found in them are not to be pressed too far. As Timothy will benefit others, so he will be helped himself, **brought up on the truths of the faith.** The Greek suggests a continual process : 'being nourished.' Timothy is to ponder constantly the true Christian principles, and derive from them, as from his daily bread, the necessary vigour for his work. It is further suggested that in the teaching of Paul **(the lessons of the good doctrine you have already followed)** the Christian message has been transmitted in its purity. The Pastoral Epistles are written on this assumption. Over against later perversions in doctrine and practice they set the genuine Pauline tradition in which Timothy had been nurtured. The word describing how Timothy had **followed** Paul's instructions is one which implies diligent study ; Luke employs it when he speaks, at the beginning of his Gospel, of his careful enquiries into the record (Luke i. 3). The writer's object here is to impress on teachers of his own day that, instead of confusing themselves with novel speculations, they ought to read and re-read the Epistles of Paul. In these they will find everything they need for the upbuilding of the spiritual life.

7 **Shut your mind against these profane, drivelling myths.** The reference is to the fictions which have been mentioned previously as ' genealogies,' religious fables which were used both by Jewish and gnostic teachers for the enforcement of their strange beliefs. They are called **profane,** to indicate that although they dealt with religious themes they had no religious value. The purely secular is always most apparent when it is coupled with the spiritual, as in Church enterprises run on

profitable commercial lines, or novels and magazines with some religious veneer. **Profane** is the Latin equivalent for the Greek word used here, and means literally 'in front of the temple' —ground which lay just outside of the holy precincts and was therefore conspicuously common. The other epithet 'old wives'' may imply that these religious myths are just as credible as the fairy-tales which grandmothers tell to children. Or perhaps it is merely a term of contempt. Those stories, supposed to convey a profound moral, are **drivelling**, made up of superstitions which none but foolish old women can believe.

It may be the mention of old women spinning cobwebs of idle fancy that suggests the contrast of a strong man in training. As an athlete drills himself constantly to maintain his physical vigour, so the Christian must **train for the religious life.** What the training consists in we are not told ; but, since ' godliness ' in these Epistles is at once devotional and practical, we must think of the drill that produces it as combining both of these elements. It must be strenuous because so much depends on it. **The training of the body is of some small service.** 8 This might also mean ' for a short time,' but the other translation is preferable, since the contrast is between a great and a small result. With a true Greek feeling the writer admits the value of physical training, but points out that it has only one object and that a very limited one ; while **religion is of service in all directions.** It has sometimes been held that the ' bodily discipline ' is that of asceticism, and that the verse thus follows up the previous allusion to the rules laid down by the false teachers. But it is that very allusion which makes such a meaning impossible. Ascetic practices have been condemned as wrong and devilish ; here it is admitted that ' bodily exercise ' has a real though minor value. We must therefore take the words in their literal sense. The training of the higher nature is contrasted with that of the body, since **it contains the promise of life both for the present and for the future.** The mention of a promise, in the New Testament, usually has reference to something promised in scripture, and the writer may here be thinking of various Old Testament passages in which life is said to be the reward of righteousness. He may also have

49

in mind the saying of Jesus in Luke xviii. 30 (' receive manifold
more in this present time, and in the world to come life everlasting '). It has sometimes been objected that in this
emphasis on the double value of religion he comes dangerously
near the type of piety which tries to ' make the best of both
worlds.' This may be so ; but it may be pleaded for him that
he merely states a fact. Religion, while it offers hope for the
hereafter, also gives a fuller meaning and a deeper happiness to
the present life.

9 At this point another **sure word** is introduced, and whether
the formula applies to what precedes or what follows is not
altogether clear. It seems most natural to look for the quoted
saying in the words before, which have all the marks of a
proverb or epigram in praise of the religious life. The verse
that follows is thus meant to explain why the sentiment quoted
10 is one that all Christians must respond to. For to this end—
i.e. to the attainment of life—**we toil and strive.** In some
manuscripts the reading is ' we suffer reproaches,' but this (as
Moffatt points out in a footnote) is out of place. The idea of
the trained athlete is taken up again. Instead of the ' corrup-
tible crown ' (i Cor. ix. 25) which rewards a victor in the
games, the Christian ' toils and wrestles '; he submits himself
to the hardest discipline in order to obtain everlasting life.
This he does **because our hope is fixed upon the living God.**
As Himself the living One, God bestows life ; and, as the living,
He is also the real and active God, not the imaginary being who
is the object of the new speculations. It is this idea which
gives point to the closing words of the passage, **who is the
Saviour of all men—of believers in particular.** The thought of
God as caring for all men has already been offered as a
reason for making prayer on behalf of all. Here it is empha-
sized as against the gnostic theory that God intends His
salvation only for a favoured class of ' spiritual men ' ; to the
writer's mind this is the very negation of that knowledge of
God which we have through Christ. But while God is the
Saviour of all, He is in a special sense the Christian's Saviour.
This addition might seem almost to cancel the main thought,
but the writer evidently intends to reinforce it. Since all men

can look to God as their Saviour, the Christian may have absolute confidence. Those who have expressly put their faith in
God can be certain of the mercy which is extended to all.

SPECIAL ADMONITIONS (iv. 11–16)

Give these orders and teach these lessons. Let no one slight ^11–^12^
    you because you are a youth, but set the believers an
    example of speech, behaviour, love, faith, and purity.
    Attend to your Scripture-reading, your preaching, and your 13
    teaching, till I come. You have a gift that came to you 14
    transmitted by the prophets, when the presbytery laid their
    hands upon you ; do not neglect that gift. Attend to these 15
    duties, let them absorb you, so that all men may note your
    progress. Watch yourself and watch your teaching ; stick 16
    to your work ; if you do that, you will save your hearers as
    well as yourself.

The previous section has dealt in a general manner with the
duty of self-discipline. While the counsels have been addressed
to Timothy, they were of such a nature as to be applicable to
all Christians. The next verses are still on the need for self-
discipline, but are meant directly for Timothy, in his character
of Church leader.

He is first enjoined to impress on others the precepts which 11
have just been laid down. Conscious that he speaks with
Paul's own authority he must allow no one to despise or 12
slight his youth ; he must be so full of his message that men will
forget that he is a young man instructing those who are much
older than himself. This reference to the youth of Timothy
is one of the indications that the Epistle cannot have been
written by Paul in the interval between a first and second
imprisonment at Rome. Timothy would then be a man of
about forty, and no one would think it presumptuous in him
to come forward as a teacher. The writer apparently meant us
to think of the letter as dating from the time of Paul's three
years' mission at Ephesus, when Timothy was still a young
man. But the admonition, though addressed to Timothy, is

intended for all young men who were called on to take responsible positions in the Church. This must have happened frequently in the early period. Like all new movements, Christianity would find its converts chiefly among the young whose minds were open to new ideas. It would be one of the chief reproaches against the new religion that it was so often represented by young men, who were expected by ancient sentiment to defer to the wisdom of their elders. Timothy is adjured to turn his very youth to account by setting an **example in speech, behaviour, love, faith, and purity.** Although a young man, he was to excel in those very qualities in which youth is wont to be deficient—gravity, prudence, consideration for others, trustworthiness, mastery over the passions.

13 **Attend to your Scripture-reading, your preaching, and your teaching, till I come.** These were the duties which the apostle himself was accustomed to discharge, and during his absence Timothy was to see that they were properly carried out. They were the chief ministerial functions in the early worship. As in the synagogue, on which the Church had modelled itself, a passage from the Bible was read to the congregation. There was as yet no Christian scripture, and the passage was taken from the Old Testament, although already (as we know from Justin) ' memoirs of Jesus ' and writings by the apostles were also read. This public reading was the more important as books were scarce and dear and the people often illiterate, so that all knowledge of the scriptures had to be obtained by hearing. The **preaching** consisted of an address, expounding the passage read, while the **teaching** would be more informal,

14 often carried out by question and answer. **Do not neglect**—or perhaps ' do not forget'; in order to do his duty boldly, Timothy must constantly remember that he has been given a full commission—**a gift that came to you transmitted by the prophets, when the presbytery laid their hands upon you.** In the Epistles of Paul the word *charisma* means a spiritual gift—i.e. a special endowment bestowed directly by the Spirit. Speaking with tongues, prophetic insight, powers of eloquence and of healing, Christian love, were ' spiritual gifts.' The word seems here to be applied to an office,

conferred by the Spirit, inasmuch as those appointed to it were designated by inspired **prophets** (mention has already been made in i. 18 of the ' prophecies ' which had led to the call of Timothy). But besides this choice by the Spirit there needed to be the formal act by which the servant of the Church was ordained. This act took the form of a ' laying on of hands ' by the whole group of elders. According to 2 Tim. ii. 6 Timothy was ordained ' by the laying on of my hands,' but there is no necessary contradiction. The aim of the second Epistle is to make Timothy the true successor of Paul, who had personally assisted in his ordination. The aim here is to assure him that his commission is fully legitimate, since all the elders had co-operated with Paul in ordaining him. It is to be noted that a word had already been coined to denote the elders in their common capacity. They acted not as a number of separate officers, but as a board.

The practice of laying on of hands was taken over by the Church from Judaism, and no doubt had its origin in primitive religious ideas. All endowments were conceived to be in some manner physical, so that they could be **transmitted** by physical contact. Some kind of electric fluid was passed from the one person to the other, and with it the given capacity. The gesture of touching was employed in acts of healing, in exorcism, in blessing, in the appointment to offices and dignities. Examples of all these are found in the Old Testament, and in each case the same idea is present; from the person in whom the virtue resides it passes, by the contact of the hands, into the recipient. Several times in the Gospels we read of Jesus laying His hands on the sick, as He did on little children when He blessed them. In the book of Acts it is assumed that the laying on of hands is an integral part of baptism, and in Heb. vi. 1 ' the doctrine of baptism and the laying on of hands ' is mentioned as one of the elementary parts of Christian instruction. That the rite continued to be used in connexion with baptism, we know from pictures in the Catacombs. It stood, apparently, for the positive transmission of the Spirit after sin had been washed away in the baptismal water. Almost from the first the laying on of hands must have been the central act in ordination, for it appears several times in the book of Acts (e.g. vi. 6; xiii. 1). We know that it was customary among the Jews in the consecration of judges, scribes, and members of the Sanhedrim, and was traced back to the laying of Moses' hands on Joshua (Num. xxvii. 18f.). The Jewish practice was adopted by the Church, and was now combined with distinctively Christian ideas. The Spirit sent by Christ was supposed to be communicated by those who already possessed it by the laying on of hands.

15   In the closing verses of the chapter the thought of a training necessary for the Christian worker as for the athlete is further developed. ' Practise these things,' like exercises that must become instinctive movements ; **let them absorb you** (lit. ' have your being in them ' ; make them your very nature), **so that all men may note your progress.** There may be a further allusion here to Timothy's youth. If men think him too young, let them at least recognize that he is always growing, alike in his spiritual life and in his practical efficiency as a Christian leader. Or the idea may be simply that of the athlete who trains so hard that you can observe him, day by day,

16 growing into a stronger man. **Watch yourself and watch your teaching.** The personal life and the teaching are purposely brought together. Timothy's power **as a** teacher will be in proportion to his consistency ; while he **is** careful about what he says, he must be equally careful to say nothing that is not borne out by his life. **Stick to the directions given ; if you do that, you will save** both **your hearers and yourself.** Perhaps there is here a reminiscence of Paul's fear ' lest when I have preached to others I myself may be a castaway ' (1 Cor. ix. 27). It is the constant danger of the religious teacher that, in his concern for those he works for, he should take himself for granted. He must therefore exercise an ever-vigilant self-discipline, remembering that his own soul is one of those which must be saved.

.   .   .   .

The earlier part of the Epistle has contained general directions with regard to the right ordering of the Church. Some instructions of a more specific nature are now given. Timothy is counselled as to the manner in which he should deal with the various groups that make up the community, older and younger members, dependants on Church bounty, fellow-officers, slaves. Nothing is said of children, presumably because they are entrusted to the guidance of their own parents (cf. iii. 4, 12 and v. 10). An attention which seems quite disproportionate is given to widows ; the section about them is, indeed, the fullest and most definite in the whole Epistle, and it has been conjectured that the writer at this point incorporates an extract from some Church manual. The treatment of widows, however, seems always to have been a matter of special difficulty to the Early Church. It was on this question that dissension first arose (Acts vi. 1), and a large space is devoted to it in later ecclesiastical writers, just as in the Pastorals. The reason no doubt is that widows were the natural recipients of charity, and the whole business of the Church funds was largely concerned with them.

The previous section closed with a reference to ' your hearers,' and this is the connecting link between the earlier and later sections of the Epistle. Interest now centres on these ' hearers,' who fall into a number of distinct classes.

DIFFERENT AGES AND SEXES (v. 1–2)

v.

Never censure an older man harshly ; appeal to him as a father. 1
  Treat younger men like brothers, older women like mothers, 2
  younger women like sisters—with perfect propriety.

In the first injunction the reference is clearly not to ' elders ' 1 in the ecclesiastical sense, but to the older men in the Christian community. They are not to be ' struck at '—a word which includes all harsh usage, either in act or speech. Even when he has to rebuke them, Timothy must address them more like a son than a superior. In like manner he must **treat younger men like brothers, older women like mothers.** To be sure, he is 2 invested with authority, and on proper occasion, as he is told later, must not hesitate to use it ; but as far as may be he must preserve the natural human relation to the various people under his charge. He must likewise treat the younger women like sisters, in ' all purity.' The most delicate of all the relations in which he was placed, as a spiritual adviser, is exquisitely touched on in a single word, which says everything.

WIDOWS (v. 3–16)

3–4 Widows in real need must be supported from the funds. (When a widow has children or grandchildren, they must learn that the first duty of religion is to their own household, and that they should make some return to those who have brought them up. In God's sight this is a commendable

5 deed.) The really forlorn widow has her hope fixed on God, night and day she is at her prayers and supplications ;

6 whereas the widow who plunges into dissipation is dead

7 before ever she dies. So lay down these rules to prevent

8 any reproach being incurred. Whoever does not provide for his own relatives, and particularly for his own family,

9 has repudiated the faith : he is worse than an infidel. No one under sixty is to be put on the church's list of widows ;

10 and she must have been only once married, she must have a reputation for good service, as a woman who has brought up children, shown hospitality, washed the feet of the saints, relieved distress, and interested herself in all good works.

11 Refuse to put young widows on the list, for when their wanton desires make them chafe against Christ, they want to

12 marry and are thus guilty of breaking their first troth to

13 Him. Besides, they become idle unconsciously[1] by gadding about from one house to another—and not merely idle but gossips and busybodies, repeating things they have no right

14 to mention. So I prefer young widows to marry again, to bear children, to look after their households, and not to

15 afford our opponents any chance of reviling us. As it is,

---

[1] I accept the conjecture λανθάνουσι for the μανθάνουσι of the canonical text, which makes the grammatical construction very awkward.

some widows have already strayed after Satan.—Any 16
believer, man or woman, who has widowed relatives, must
give them relief ; the church is not to be burdened with
them ; she has to relieve the widows who really need relief.

The section falls into two parts : (1) the duties which the
Church owes to widows ; (2) the duties which widows owe to
the Church. But these two aspects of the subject merge in
one another, so that no sharp division can be made. The whole
passage is beset with a peculiar difficulty which would not be
felt by the first readers, but can now be met only by conjecture. What was the status assigned to widows ? That they
were entitled to assistance is clear ; but were they required to
discharge certain duties in return for this assistance ? They
are spoken of sometimes as merely widows in need of charity,
sometimes as if they were an official class. Probably it was
expected that they would perform some service. Since they
were free from household duties, it was only right that they
should occupy themselves with Church work which could not
fairly be thrown on busy wives and mothers. But there were
evidently some of the widows who had a sort of official status.
They were not on the footing of ' elders,' since they took no
part in the government of the Church ; yet they supervised
the female members in much the same way as the elders were
responsible for the men. In this passage, therefore, the word
' widows ' is employed in a technical as well as in its ordinary
sense. Later manuals of Church order (e.g. that of Hippolytus)
make mention of ' widows ' as a regular group of Church
officials, and a similar group seems to be contemplated in this
chapter.

The section begins with a precept the drift of which has 3
been disputed, but is probably what Moffatt makes it in his
translation. It reads literally ' Honour widows who are truly
so '—i.e. who have not merely lost their husbands, but are
quite alone in the world. They are entitled to the special
regard of the Church, and the word ' honour ' is deliberately
used, in order to suggest that reverence is due to all who are
in affliction. But it carries with it, as we can gather from

what follows, the idea of active assistance. By a play on the Greek word ' honour,' which can also mean ' pay ' (as in our own word '. honorarium '), the writer declares that a pension should be conferred on widows as their natural right. At the same time he is anxious that the charity of the Church, which had so many calls to answer, should not be misused ; and the rules which follow are meant to restrict the payment to cases of real need. Those only are to be assisted by the Church

4 who are destitute of any other help. **When a widow has children or grandchildren** (lit. ' descendants '), **they must learn that the first duty of religion is to their own household, and that they should make some return to those who have brought them up** (lit. ' to their progenitors '). The thought is expressed confusedly, so much so that it may be understood in two quite different senses. **They must learn** may refer to the widows, who are thus told that if they have families of their own they are not to seek Church work, with the payment attached to it, since they have plenty to do at home. But the whole context points to the other meaning. If the widow has ' descendants ' (the word is purposely chosen so as to include all immediate relations) it is their duty first—i.e. before application is made to the Church—to do what they can for her. This interpretation is confirmed by two details : (1) The phrase **duty of religion** (lit. ' to act piously ') applies more naturally to children than to parents. We speak of filial, but not of parental piety. (2) The other phrase **make a return** can hardly mean anything else than to recompense parents for what they have done. It has been argued that the widow ' makes a return to her progenitors ' by the care which she, in turn, bestows on her descendants ; but this is much too subtle and artificial. So the rule is laid down that a widow's own family should be the first to help her. The demand is in itself a reasonable one, and it also has a religious sanction, for it is 'acceptable in the sight of God,' who gave the express commandment ' honour thy

5 father and mother.' **The really forlorn widow has her hope fixed on God :** since there is none but God to help her, she has a full right to ask the Church, which is God's community, to take her under its protection. Yet here again the Church must

be safeguarded. The widow who indeed hopes in God is at her prayers and supplications night and day. She attends both to her public and her private devotions; she is manifestly a religious woman and a genuine member of the Church. Whereas the widow who plunges into dissipation is dead while 6 living. This must not be taken as a general reflection on self-indulgence as a living death. The word ' living ' bears the technical sense of vital connexion with the Church; the writer says in effect that a loose-living widow is only a nominal Christian. She professes to be a Church member, but is like the branch in the Fourth Gospel which bears no fruit and is cut off and withers (John xv. 6). To women who do not in any real sense belong to it, the Church owes no obligation.

So lay down these rules ; not ' the following rules ' but those 7 which have just been stated. Care is to be taken that both widows and their families may incur no reproach—i.e. no suspicion that they are using selfishly the money which might have helped those in real need. A word is added to make it 8 clear that families which allow their widows to take charity from the Church are more to blame than the widows themselves. But whoever does not provide for his own relations (lit. ' his nearest and peculiarly his own ') has repudiated the faith. The thought is not merely that charity begins at home— which is usually made the pretext for helping no one but our immediate friends. It is rather that the very meaning of Christianity is to love all men, and that no one who neglects his own kindred has any part whatever in the gospel. He is worse than an infidel ; for the heathen at least show affection to their own families, although their sense of human obligation extends no further. The Christian who has no regard for his kinsfolk does not even go so far as the heathen ; and he is all the more culpable as the standard he professes is so much higher.

In the passage that follows, the thought passes from ordinary widows to those who employ their leisure in performing stated duties for the Church. No one under sixty is to be put on the 9 church's list of widows. Two terms with a technical meaning are here employed. The Church kept a ' list ' of persons who were not only members but actively engaged in its service. Among those persons in the catalogue some were entered as ' widows,' and they had to be carefully selected. They were not merely widows in the ordinary sense, or widows who had no one to support them, for in this case the only qualification would be that of genuine need. It cannot be supposed, for instance, that the Church would refuse help to a widow if she was under sixty, for this restriction would be simply cruel if the question were one of charity ; the widows in direst need would generally be the younger ones, who were left with small children. Quite evidently the point of the restriction is that for certain duties the Church required women who could be counted on to devote themselves wholly to the work. At the age of sixty they would have given up all thought of re-marriage ; they would have little inclination to take up with worldly pleasures and interests.

Along with suitable age they needed to have a proved Christian character. A woman placed on the list must have been **only once married**. The bishop, according to iii. 2, had to be ' husband of one wife,' apparently in the sense that he was to be a man of pure moral life. This may be all that is implied in the requirement that the widow must have been ' wife of one husband.' But ancient sentiment allowed a special credit to the widow who refrained from second marriage. A well-known biblical instance is that of Anna the prophetess in Luke ii. 36. Thus the meaning seems to be that a woman who had been for some time a widow and had not re-married, had shown by that alone that her moral character was high. Besides this negative proof, **she must have a reputation for good service**—of the kind which would fall to her as a Church worker. Examples are given of the service required. She must have **brought up children**, not necessarily children of her own ; the meaning is simply that she must be a ' motherly ' person. Her duties as a Church ' widow ' would be largely concerned with children, and it was important that she should have a real aptitude for dealing with them. She must have **shown hospitality**. Here again there is

60

a hint of the duties she would have to perform. One of the offices to which the Early Church devoted itself was that of entertaining travellers, and this would be largely in the hands of the ' widows.' They needed to be women who were known to have the hospitable spirit. The further reference to washing the feet of the saints may also imply hospitality ; the first kindness shown to a stranger was to see that his feet were washed after the dusty and toilsome journey. But the idea of humility is added to that of welcome. Women were needed who would perform the lowliest duties on behalf of others, in the spirit which Christ Himself had taught by His example (John xiii. 14). She must have relieved distress, and interested herself in all good works. Instead of further specifying the virtues required, the writer now speaks in comprehensive terms ; the Church must make sure, before enrolling a widow, that she has the right disposition for the work. Interested herself (lit. ' followed up ') may carry a special emphasis. It is not enough to have acted now and then from a generous impulse ; there must be evidence of a consistent habit of charity. Refuse to put young widows on the list—i.e. widows 11 under the age of sixty. For their wanton desires alienate them from Christ (lit. ' they grow restive against Christ '). A word is used which denotes an excess of energy ; our word ' stren- uous ' is from the same root. The suggestion is that the younger widows become impatient of the staid routine imposed on them. Against Christ is only another way of saying ' against Christian service.' In a moment of ardour they undertake a work which soon begins to bore them, and they want to marry and thus are guilty (lit. incur the judgment) of breaking their 12 original pledge. They had come under a promise to give themselves wholly to Church duties, and now wish to go back to ordinary life. The ' judgment ' which they incur need not be that of God. Nothing seems to be meant except that a reproach clings to them ever afterwards. One is reminded of the words in Rev. ii. 6, 8, ' thou hast left thy first love,' but the resemblance seems to be accidental. Besides, they become 13 idle unconsciously. Moffatt here accepts a conjecture which overcomes a serious grammatical difficulty by the change of a

single letter. But the change has no support in the manuscripts, and it is safer to make the best we can of the Greek as
it stands. It may possibly mean ' they learn by idleness '—
i.e. they acquire the loose habits and notions which come to
idle people. More probably we ought to translate ' they learn
to be idlers.' The idiom used, though rare, is not impossible,
and the writer's point seems clearly to be that they grow idle,
not that they do so unconsciously. **Gadding about from one
house to another,** i.e. making their Church work a mere pretext
for poking into the affairs of their neighbours. **And not
merely idle but gossips and busybodies.** The picture is so true
to life that it explains itself, though it might apply just as
well to older widows as to the younger ones. Perhaps the
suggestion is that by the nature of the work required of them
the younger widows may be led to contract bad habits, while
the older women, whose characters are already formed, will
not succumb so easily to the temptations put in their way.

14 **So I prefer young widows to marry, to bear children, to
look after their households.** The position here adopted is
different from that of Paul in 1 Cor. vii. 25f. Although Paul
does not forbid marriage, he holds that it is better for the
unmarried to remain so, in view of the great crisis which is
imminent. When the Pastorals were written, the hope of the
Parousia had failed ; Christians are now advised to adapt
themselves to ordinary conditions and to provide for the
continuance of the Church as part of the present order. On
the other hand, there is a striking difference between the
position here and that of the later Church. In the course of
the second and third centuries, as a result of the ascetic ideas
which had become prevalent, an increasing value was placed
on celibacy. Here, the state of marriage is deemed preferable
to the other. The ascetic attitude has been condemned in
earlier passage (iv. 3), and now even widows who are of suitable
age are advised to follow the course which is more natural.
The common sense which is a feature of these Epistles is
nowhere more apparent. A reason which is added is also
characteristic : **not to afford our opponents any chance of
reviling us.** The writer is always anxious that the Church

should stand well with the surrounding world. He is aware
that no charges against the new religion were more effective
than those which touched the character of Christian women. 15
These malicious reports, he has to admit, are occasionally
true ; for **some widows have already turned after Satan.**
Elsewhere the expression is used for following wrong doctrines
(2 Tim. ii. 26 ; iii. 6f.) ; but it can hardly have such a meaning
here. To the outside world, whose judgments are in question,
one variety of Christian belief would be much the same as
another ; in his famous book against Christianity, written
probably in the same age as the Pastorals, the pagan Celsus
takes for granted that gnostic doctrines are held by the whole
Church. ' Turning after Satan ' must here apply to the
frivolous or immoral habits into which some of the women
had fallen, through abusing the liberty permitted them by the
gospel.

The next verse seems to come in abruptly, and has strayed, 16
in the opinion of some commentators, from its right place
after verses 4 or 8. **Any believer, man or woman, who has
widowed relatives, must give them relief.** The best attested
reading is ' any believing woman,' but the previous passage
clearly requires all relatives, whether men or women, to look
after their own widows. Moffatt has therefore preferred the
reading which is more in keeping with the context, and apparently with common sense. But perhaps the reference to ' any
believing woman ' is intentional, and explains why the present
verse has been added in what seems its wrong place. The
writer has forbidden the enrolment of younger widows, but
now points out how they can do a real service for the Church,
even though they are not official workers. It would sometimes happen that the younger widow could assist her aged
mother or mother-in-law ; and if she had money left her, or
the means of earning it, she could take some needy widow as
her particular charge, so that the Church would not be burdened. An excellent illustration is afforded by the inscription
on an early Christian tombstone at Rome : ' Erected by her
daughter to the good Regina, her widowed mother, who lived
a widow for sixty years and was never a burden to the Church.'

THE TREATMENT OF PRESBYTERS (v. 17–21)

17 Presbyters who are efficient presidents are to be considered
worthy of ample remuneration, particularly those who
18 have the task of preaching and teaching : Scripture says,
You must not muzzle an ox when he is treading the grain,
and, *A workman deserves his wages.*

19 Never let any charge be brought against a presbyter, unless it
20 is certified by two or three witnesses. Those who are
guilty of sin you should expose in public, to overawe the
others.

21 In the presence of God and the Lord Jesus Christ and the elect
angels, I adjure you to be unprejudiced in carrying out
these orders ; be absolutely impartial.

Directions are now given as to the oversight which Timothy,
as presiding officer, should exercise with regard to the presbyters. The matter was a delicate one, since the presbyters
themselves held a place of high authority in the Church
It was specially difficult when the presbyter had made himself
liable to discipline at the hands of a younger man.

17   All presbyters had the task of presiding over Church
affairs ; but those who laboured hard in their office were to
have **ample remuneration** (lit. ' double honour,' as compared
with the others). According to one view, which is accepted
by Moffatt, ' honour ' is only a euphemism for pay (cf. v. 3).
This meaning is no doubt included, though it may not be the
whole one. An elder had to give a large part of his time to
the work of the Church, and was entitled to be relieved, in
some degree, from the need of earning his living. No slight on
the other elders is implied in ' those who have served or who
rule well.' There would be some who admittedly did the work
which entailed most time and exertion, and they had a right
not only to more recompense, but to more esteem. This was
particularly true of **those who have the task of preaching and
teaching.** All elders were expected to take some share in

teaching (iii. 2 ; Titus i. 8, 9), but there were those who had special gifts for this kind of work and were constantly engaged in it. That their labour should be duly recognized is proved 18 by two sayings, which are both quoted as scripture. One of them—' Thou shalt not muzzle the ox '—is from Deut. xxv. 4, and is cited by Paul, with a similar application, in 1 Cor. ix. 9. The other—' a workman deserves his wages '—is not found in the Old Testament, but occurs in Luke x. 7 as a saying of Jesus. Some have supposed that the writer, by a slip of memory, has assigned this saying also to the Old Testament ; but he evidently had before him the passage (1 Cor. ix. 9–14) in which Paul alludes to both the sayings and expressly speaks of this one as from ' the Lord.' It may thus be inferred that when the Pastorals were written the words of Jesus had come to be placed on the same level as scripture. From this it does not necessarily follow that the present Gospels were known to the writer and quoted by him. He may have had before him one or more of the brief collections of Sayings which were current in the Church, long before the making of regular Gospels was taken in hand. It is significant, however, that in his references to Jesus' teaching he shows close agreement with the Gospel of Luke, and was probably acquainted with it. The book of Acts was certainly known to him, and we fairly assume that he had access to the complete work of which it was the second volume

Transition is now made from the rewarding of elders who have deserved well of the Church to the censuring of those who have failed in their duty. **Never let any charge be brought 19 against a presbyter, unless it is certified by two or three witnesses.** The maxim that no man must be condemned except ' at the mouth of two or three witnesses,' which is quoted several times in the New Testament (Matt. xviii. 16 ; 2 Cor. xiii. 1), was the cardinal principle of Jewish legal procedure (Deut. xix. 15). The Jew enjoyed a protection almost unique under ancient codes of justice, by this proviso that nothing could be proved against him unless several witnesses fully concurred in their testimony. Some would interpret the words here as meaning that an accused elder must be examined

' in the presence of ' two or three witnesses ; but it is hardly possible that a maxim so familiar should be strained from its natural meaning, and that honoured servants of the Church should be put on public trial whenever there was any complaint against them. The meaning of the verse is simply that the elders must not be at the mercy of any ill-natured individual ; they must enjoy at least as much protection as was granted to everybody under Jewish Law. When the fault is proved, however, by several independent witnesses, there must be no attempt to hush it up, out of regard for the man 20 himself or the dignity of his office. He is to be exposed in public (lit. ' in the presence of all '). This is sometimes explained as meaning ' before all the other elders,' but if the exposure went no further there would be something of the secrecy which it is the aim of the writer to prevent. The elders as a body would do what they could to shield the reputation of one of their number. It was necessary that when one of the trusted leaders had been proved wanting, his error should have full publicity **to overawe the others.** If the elders were to be examples of Christian living, their faults 21 also must serve for general admonition. From what follows it is evident that scandals had sometimes arisen from the preferential treatment dealt out to elders. **In the presence of God and the Lord Jesus Christ and the elect angels, I adjure you**—i.e. with the utmost earnestness and solemnity. It is only here in the New Testament that mention is made of ' elect angels,' and the phrase seems to be taken from the apocalyptic writings (e.g. Enoch xxxix. 1). It may mean the angels who had kept their faith when the others fell ; or perhaps the angels who were specially chosen to surround the throne of God on the Day of Judgment. There is possibly a reminiscence of Jesus' own saying that He would disown His unworthy servants when He came ' in His glory and that of the Father and the holy angels ' (Luke ix. 26). **Be unprejudiced in carrying out these orders ; be absolutely impartial.** The caution is twofold : ' do not pre-judge a case, admitting doubtful charges because you do not like the man ; and do not be lenient on any personal grounds, when a case is proved.'

66

Some Additional Cautions (v. 22-25)

Never be in a hurry to ordain a presbyter ; do not make your- 22
self responsible for the sins of another man—keep your
own life pure.[1] Some people's sins are notorious and 24
call for judgment, but in some cases sin only comes out
afterwards. Good works are equally conspicuous ; and 25
even when they are not, they cannot escape notice for
ever.

The section is in several ways a difficult one : (1) The
connexion with what goes before is by no means clear. (2) The
warning with regard to undue haste can be variously explained.
(3) The verse on drinking of wine appears so irrelevant that
it has sometimes been set down as misplaced or interpolated.
It is unnecessary, however, to look for any close sequence in
the verses. Now that he has finished the main part of his
instructions the writer throws in a few miscellaneous warnings
by way of appendix ; they may have been suggested by the
previous passage, but are attached to it quite loosely.

Never be in a hurry to ordain (lit. ' to lay hands on any man '). 22
Since the earlier part of the chapter has been concerned with
elders, deacons, and other officials the verse seems to be a
general reflection on the appointment of Church workers.
They must not be ordained before thorough investigation has
been made, for something in their past record may come to
light which will cause bitter regret to those who have chosen
them. This is plainly the meaning of the words that follow :
do not make yourself responsible for the sins of another man.
He who ordains has stood surety for those whom he has admitted, and, if they are unworthy, he has, in some manner,
implicated himself in their sins. When you set a bad man
to some important work, you must share the blame for any
mischief he may do. It has been suggested, however, that the

---

[1] The words, ' Give up being a total abstainer ; take a little wine for the
sake of your stomach and your frequent attacks of illness,' which follow, are
either a marginal gloss or misplaced.

67

reference is not to elders but simply to penitents. We know that early in the third century, when numbers of Christians had lapsed under stress of persecution, they were readmitted after due repentance by a procedure in which a laying on of hands was the crowning act. The two verses, 24 and 25, are evidently meant to explain verse 22, and might seem to be more applicable to penitents than to elders. But if the practice of restoring penitents by laying on of hands was in use when these Epistles were written, it would be particularly fitting in the case of penitent elders. A ceremony was followed in which their ordination was, so to speak, given back to them. The passage may therefore be a postscript to that on discipline of elders : ' When an elder has been condemned, do not be over-hasty in restoring him, for he may still be more guilty than you know.' This meaning, however, is unsatisfactory for several reasons : (1) Laying on of hands is connected in these Epistles with ordination, and would not suddenly be mentioned here with a quite different purpose. (2) In taking back a penitent you only need to assure yourself that his repentance is genuine. Would the father of the Prodigal Son have been morally culpable if his son had fallen again ? (3) In the case of Church penitents it was past sins that were in question, but the reference here is to sins which may be committed in the future. So the passage can be best explained as alluding not to penitence but to ordination. ' Do not be hasty in ordaining an elder. Make perfectly sure that the man you ordain is worthy of the office, for if he turns out to be a hypocrite or impostor you will be responsible for the mischief which he does.' As everywhere in the Epistles the writer is anxious that none but the best men should hold office in the Church.

Keep your own life pure is often taken as part of the foregoing verse, repeating the caution to stand clear of another man's sins. But it is better understood as an independent sentence, with a strong emphasis on ' yourself.' ' Choose good men to help you, but be certain above all that you are yourself
23 a good man.' A connexion can thus be seen for the advice which follows, and which at first sight appears so out of place that Moffatt has omitted it from the text, although it is found

in all the manuscripts. ' Be no longer a water-drinker, but use a little wine for your digestion and your frequent illnesses.' Timothy has been exhorted to purity, but is reminded that this does not mean asceticism, which has been strongly condemned in the previous chapter (iv. 1-5). Occasion is taken again to insist that whatever is really helpful to man's well-being may be used with a good conscience. It has to be noted that the verse is meant, not to advocate the use of wine, but to protest against a type of doctrine which would rule out the whole physical side of man's life as evil. Taken in this sense it helps to illustrate the admirable sanity which is everywhere characteristic of this writer. He recognizes that the body has its rights, and is impatient with saints who will not behave like normal human beings.

After this brief parenthesis, the question of forming right estimates of men's characters is resumed. **Some people's sins** 24 **are notorious, and call for judgment** (lit. ' go before to judgment,' not waiting for condemnation but crying out for it). ' Some men they follow after '—their sins need to be dragged to light. The **judgment** may be that of Timothy and his assessors ; they will have to deal with some men whose characters are plainly bad, while others can only be exposed by searching back into their past. But it is better to understand the judgment as that of God. There would be little point in advising Timothy against men whom he would recognize at once as evildoers. The meaning is that at the final judgment some men will show plainly what they are ; others will not have their secret wickedness disclosed until they stand before God. In like manner **good works are** sometimes 25 **conspicuous; and even when they are not, they cannot** be hidden. From this second verse it seems evident that the reference is to God's judgment. The most careful human scrutiny cannot be relied on to discover the secret goodness in many a man's life; it is only God who will finally do justice to those whom their fellow-men have sorely misunderstood. The two verses together are meant to impress on Timothy the complexities of human nature. All proper enquiries must be made in order that the right men may be chosen for the work of the Church.

Yet our judgments at best are often mistaken. There are plausible characters who sadly deceive us : there are others of whom we feel very doubtful, and who will yet, in the end, receive the approval of God.

DUTIES OF SLAVES (vi. 1–2)

vi.

1 Let all servants who are under the yoke of slavery remember that their masters are entitled to perfect respect—otherwise it will be a scandal to the Name of God and to our doctrine.

2 Those who have Christian believers as their masters must not take liberties with them because they are brothers ; they must be all the better servants because those who get the good of their service are believers and beloved.

In these two verses (which properly belong to the previous paragraph) the counsels with regard to different classes of Church members are brought to a conclusion. It was plainly impossible to lay down rules for all sections of the community, but there was one which could not be overlooked, since it constantly raised very serious problems. The principles of the gospel were obviously in conflict with the institution of slavery, which was an integral part of all the social and economic life of the time. In every Christian Church there were slaves, and within the Church they were treated as brethren, on a full equality with their masters. How was this equality to be harmonized with their inferior status in ordinary life ? The problem was really insoluble, and it was the sense of this conflict between religious freedom and civil bondage which finally brought about the abolition of slavery. At the outset, however, the Church had to adapt itself to the existing conditions, for any open protest would have been futile, and would have led either to social chaos or to the extinction of the Church. Rules had to be devised whereby the slave might preserve his religious standing while remaining in servitude.

1 **All servants who are under the yoke of slavery.** On the face of it this description is tautological, and some would take it as

applying to Christian slaves who were under heathen masters, and who therefore bore a double yoke. Undoubtedly these slaves, compelled often to do work which revolted their conscience, were placed in a terrible position, and the Church was often perplexed as to how it should advise them. Yet the phrase ' under a yoke ' cannot be restricted in this manner, and perhaps is meant to impress on slaves that their condition is not peculiar; to be sure, they are ' servants ' in the most obvious sense, but most men are under some kind of bondage. They are to remember that their masters are entitled to perfect respect. Frankly acknowledging their inferior position, they must conduct themselves in the proper way. There was always a danger that Christian slaves, conscious of their inward liberty, should adopt an insolent manner, and this was to be avoided ; otherwise it will be a scandal to the Name of God and to our doctrine. Here, as elsewhere, the writer is concerned for the reputation of the new religion in the outside world. Its progress might be fatally hindered if an impression got abroad that it tended to the dissolution of society. This would certainly happen if it were noted that slaves, as soon as they became Christians, showed themselves rude and unmanageable. A special caution is given to those who have 2 Christian masters, not to take liberties with them because they are brothers. A situation is here hinted at which must often have been embarrassing, and which has its counterpart to-day in some missionary lands, where Christian settlers are apt to prefer servants who are not Christians. They must be all the better servants because those who get the good of their service are believers and beloved. The Greek sentence is so constructed that it may bear either of two contrary meanings : (1) The latter part of it may refer to the slaves ; as brethren to their masters, and receiving every kindness at their hands, they are to render better service. (2) It may refer (as in our translation) to the masters. From every point of view this seems to be preferable. The slaves are to serve the more cheerfully when their masters happen to be Christians like themselves. Both masters and slaves are reminded, by a delicate turn of phrase, that the service is not to be considered a mere matter of

necessity. Masters are to think of their servants as bene-
factors ; servants are to feel that in their daily toil they have
the opportunity to do good to others.

THE DANGER OF FALSE TEACHING (vi. 2–10)

2–3 This is what you are to teach and preach. Anyone who teaches
novelties and refuses to fall in with the sound words of our
Lord Jesus Christ, and the doctrine that tallies with godli-
4   ness, is a conceited, ignorant creature, with a morbid
passion for controversy and argument which only leads to
5   envy, dissension, insults, insinuations, and constant friction
between people who are depraved in mind and deprived of
6   the Truth. They imagine religion is a paying concern. As
indeed it is—rich profit, provided that it goes with a con-
7   tented spirit—for we bring nothing into the world, and we
8   can take nothing out of it ; if we have food and clothes, we
9   must be content with that. Those who are eager to be rich
get tempted and trapped in many senseless and pernicious
propensities, that drag men down to ruin and destruction.
10   For love of money is the root of all mischief ; it is by aspiring to be rich that certain individuals have gone astray from
the faith and found themselves pierced with many a pang of
remorse.

All the particular injunctions have now been given ; the
rest of the Epistle consists of general counsels, based on what
has been said already. Verses 8–10 are in the main negative,
condemning the vain ideas and habits which for many have
taken the place of true ' godliness.' From verse 11 to the end a
positive note is struck; Timothy is reminded of those great
practical truths which he must insist on, and by which alone
all forms of error can be overcome.

2   The opening words, this is what you are to teach and preach,
have sometimes been taken as the conclusion of the passage
before ; but it is better to read them as introductory to what
follows. The writer is now to gather up into one final exhortation the ideas he has tried to enforce, and he begins by

72

emphasizing what he means to say : **Anyone who teaches novelties and does not fall in with** or rather ' attend to ' (the word means literally ' to approach,' in the sense of going up to something with a set purpose—e.g. a doctor going up to his patient, a traveller making for a spring) the business with which the Christian must occupy himself—i.e. **the sound words, the words of our Lord.** Right doctrine is again described as ' healthy,' the normal and vigorous type of faith in contrast to the morbid fancies of those who deviate into strange paths. It is doubtful whether **the words of our Lord** mean words which He has spoken or which have been said about Him. Paul invariably thinks of the message concerning Christ when he speaks of the ' word ' or ' gospel ' of Christ ; and the allusion to ' healthy words ' would likewise suggest words which deal with the right subject, not with vain abstractions, but with Christ Himself. At the same time the Epistle dates from the period in which the Gospels were being written, to satisfy the growing interest in the actual sayings of Jesus. The writer may well have these sayings in mind when he goes on to speak of **the doctrine which tallies with godliness**—i.e. which constitutes the one true norm of Christian conduct and belief. The man who neglects it is **conceited** (lit. ' has been filled with smoke ' ; he ' knows nothing, but is diseased with problems and verbal disputes '). This description is suggested by the reference to ' healthy words.' He who departs from them becomes spiritually sick. His mind is in a daze. He has no real knowledge, but wanders like a delirious man in a labyrinth of doubt and fancy, **which only leads to envy, dissension, insults, insinuations, and constant friction.** The trouble begins intellectually, but ends in a pitiable moral condition. It has often been noticed that the partisans of some eccentric theory, in religion or politics, are shortly at daggers drawn with one another. Each one tries to outbid his neighbour. The fight is all about nothing, and for that reason it seems to grow ever more bitter. The writer is evidently describing from the life this phenomenon as he had observed it in some of the heretical coteries of his day, and he suggests the cause of it. Those sectaries are **depraved** (or rather ' corrupted ') **in mind and**

4

5

73

deprived of the Truth—that is to say, they have entirely lost sight of reality and their minds have fallen into disorder. Like patients in a fever they see everything out of proportion, and grow irritated over trifles. Truth has become so meaningless to them that **they imagine religion is a paying concern.** This is the final degradation into which those false teachers fall. With all their pretension to have reached some higher kind of religion, they are able to see nothing in religion but a means of gain. The general meaning is plain, but it is doubtful whether the religion in question is their own or that of others. Do they use the piety of their neighbours in order to make money out of them ? Or do they cultivate a pious mode of life for the sake of profit ? Both kinds of religious imposture have been familiar in every age ; but the words that follow would seem to point to the second meaning. The false teachers are to all appearance religious, but behind their religion there is a sordid and earthly motive. Perhaps the reference is to the fees they demanded (after the manner of philosophical tutors of the time) in return for religious instruction. Or the meaning may be more general. A reputation for high religious character has always been an asset for the man who aims at worldly power and success ; one has only to think of financiers and politicians of our own time who have learned that secret. But the writer proceeds to show that such men have woefully perverted a true

6 principle. Religion is indeed profitable **provided it goes with a contented spirit.** The word here used for **a contented spirit** was one taken over by Christianity from the Stoics, who held that the ' wise man ' must feel himself independent of earthly accidents. Paul could thus say that in whatever state he might be he was ' self-sufficient ' (Phil. iv. 11) ; he had inner resources on which he could depend even when he was poor and in prison. So here it is implied that religion does not begin to yield its true reward until we have learned to be indifferent to worldly gains. We need to realize that they

7 have no value, **for we bring nothing into the world, and we can take nothing out of it.** The ordinary Greek text reads, ' because we can take nothing out,' and attempts have been made to explain this as meaning that our nakedness when we

leave the world is proof that we brought nothing in. But the fact that we were born with nothing is self-evident, and, even if it were not, it would not be proved by our taking nothing away. There seems little doubt that a superfluous word has crept into the Greek and has spoiled the obvious sense. If we have food and clothes, we must be content with 8 that. The word translated ' clothes ' is a comprehensive one, including all necessary shelter and covering. Life, the writer would say, is only a brief sojourn ; what object can there be in heaping up material gain ? Those who are eager to be rich 9 are like animals which are lured by their greed off the way of safety and fall into the traps laid for them. So in the quest for riches there are traps which drag men down (lit. ' plunge ' or ' sink ' them) to ruin and destruction. The two words may be used to denote loss here and loss hereafter. More likely the double phrase is meant only to lay strong emphasis on the idea that pursuit of gain is sure to bring its own punishment. For love of money is the root of all mischief. Since the article 10 before root is wanting in the Greek, it has been supposed that the writer means ' one of the roots ' ; but there can be little doubt that the stronger judgment is intended. In ethical treatises of the time we meet not infrequently with the same idea, expressed sometimes in much the same words—e.g. ' all evils can be traced back to the desire for money.' The author of the Epistle may be quoting a current proverb, to which he gives a new significance as he adds the reflection that by aspiring to be rich some have gone astray from the faith. Even heathen morality could find in covetousness the chief motive of crime, but from the Christian point of view its worst evil was spiritual. More than anything else it destroyed a man's religion. Moffatt may be right in translating ' some ' as certain individuals, definite people who, to the writer's knowledge, had suffered this moral disaster, and found them- selves pierced with many a pang of remorse (lit. ' with many pains '). The pains which are thus coupled with loss of faith cannot be merely the anxieties which attend on money- making. They must rather be understood in the light of the previous reference to ' utter ruin.' The covetous man is

HE   75

compelled to realize in the end that he has forfeited the true good of life for a little material gain. So a natural transition is made to the next section.

THE TRUE AIMS OF THE CHRISTIAN LIFE (vi. 11–16)

11 Shun that, O man of God, aim at integrity, godliness, faith,
12 love, stedfastness, modesty ; fight in the good fight of the faith, secure that life eternal to which you were called when you voiced the good confession in presence of many
13 witnesses. In presence of God who is the Life of all, and of Christ Jesus who testified to the good confession before
14 Pontius Pilate, I charge you to keep your commission free from stain, free from reproach, till the appearance of our
15 Lord Jesus Christ—which will be brought about in due time by that blessed and only Sovereign, King of kings and
16 Lord of lords, who alone has immortality, who dwells in light that no one can approach, whom no man ever has seen or can see. To Him be honour and eternal dominion : Amen.

11   The exhortation is addressed to Timothy personally, as one who holds responsible office in the Church ; but it is meant for all Christians. A professed leader stands for the ideals which all are seeking to follow. It is for this reason that Timothy is called **man of God**. The phrase is an Old Testament one, and is used of prophets who act in the name of God (Deut. xxxiii. 1 ; 1 Sam. ii. 27 ; 1 Kings xvii. 24 ; 2 Kings iv. 7). But it is a comprehensive term which may be applied to all who offer themselves for God's service. As the pattern of all these ' God's men,' the Church leader is to avoid covetousness and aim at **integrity, godliness, faith, love, stedfastness, modesty** (lit. ' gentleness of feeling '). It is to be noted that faith and love, which for Paul include everything, are here regarded as specific virtues, which need to be combined
12 with patience and meekness. **Fight in the good fight of the faith.** A word is used which means strictly a wrestling match. From

Paul onwards Christian teachers drew one of their favourite comparisons from the athletic games, so much so that the term ' athlete ' was often employed for ' Christian.' This metaphor is followed up in the next words : ' lay hold of the eternal life.' This is the prize which will finally be given to the good ' athlete,' but in the struggle to obtain it he is grasping or securing it even now. ' Eternal life ' in these Epistles has thus something of the same meaning as it has in the Fourth Gospel ; it is the real life which will continue and be perfected after death, but which is already a present possession in the believer. To this life Timothy had been called when he made **the good confession in the presence of many witnesses.** The reference is to baptism, in which the believer made his confession or ' declaration,' consisting originally in the words, ' Jesus is Lord ' (Rom. x. 9 ; 1 Cor. xii. 3 ; Phil. ii. 11). It is called **the good** or noble **confession,** since the Christian life itself has just been called the good fight. This highest enterprise to which a man can devote himself is begun and made possible by the confession made at baptism. In a later time baptism became little more than a formality, to which all who were born into the Christian empire submitted as a matter of course. But when the Pastorals were written, baptism was still an act of high resolve, like a soldier's oath to spend his life for his country. Timothy is reminded of the promise which he had made, and of the ardour which inspired him when he entered on his Christian service. He had done so in the presence of all his fellow-Christians, who can testify against him if he breaks his faith. Besides the human witnesses, God and Christ were present, and before 13 them Timothy is now adjured to stand true to his solemn obligations. In the whole passage which follows there is a suggestion of the Apostles' Creed, and this is probably no matter of accident. The Creed was developed by successive expansions, from the simple confession ' Jesus is Lord,' and it may be inferred that the process had already begun when these Epistles were written. Along with his faith in Christ the convert had to declare his belief in the true God, **the Life of all** (lit. ' who sustains all things in life '). He had also to declare

77

that Jesus had truly lived and died. This became necessary in the days of docetic heresy, when the historical reality of the Saviour's life was often denied. Perhaps in the present passage the Greek preposition should be understood as in the Apostles' Creed, ' suffered under Pontius Pilate '—i.e. died a real death, in a year of history which can be positively dated. More likely, however, we should translate, with Moffatt, **who testified to the good confession before Pontius Pilate.** The writer is thinking, not so much of the fact that Christ died, as of the manner in which He had done so. Brought before the governor, as Christians still were in the writer's day, He had shown an unflinching courage, and had thereby given an example which His people were bound to follow. What was the ' confession ' which Christ made before Pilate ? Some have found it in His admission that He was the true Messiah. More likely we are not to understand the ' confession ' in any definite sense. What is impressed on us is simply the fortitude with which Jesus was faithful unto death, and this is described in language that might be used of a martyr, refusing to deny his Lord.

After Timothy is thus reminded of the fidelity to which he 14 was bound by his confession, he is charged to keep his **commission** (lit. ' the commandment ') **free from stain, free from reproach.** The reference (as Moffatt indicates) is not to some specific injunction laid on Timothy at his baptism, but to the whole duty with which he was entrusted. He must discharge it in such a manner that no one can point to anything that has been neglected or slackly done **till the appearance of our Lord Jesus Christ.** Elsewhere in the Epistles the **appearance** (lit. ' the epiphany ') is the coming of Christ to earth. Here it is His return in glory, when He will admit to His Kingdom those who had served Him faithfully. Paul had anticipated that he would himself survive to witness this glorious return. At the later date the hope had become remote, although it was still a living part of the Christian ' confession.' There is no indication here that the Johannine conception of an inward coming of Christ to 'His own' had now taken the place of the literal expectation of the early days. Yet the date of the

Lord's appearance is now left indefinite. It has been deter- 15 mined by God, who will bring it about in due time (lit. ' in His own times ').

A doxology follows which is more akin to the hymns of praise in Revelation than to the doxologies of Paul. Not improbably it is suggested by a Christian hymn, modelled on the liturgy of the synagogue. The titles ascribed to God, **blessed and only Sovereign, King of kings and Lord of lords,** have analogies in the later Jewish literature (1 and 2 Maccabees, Ecclesiasticus, Enoch) rather than in the Old Testament. It is not necessary to see in these titles an assertion of the Divine power over against that of the earthly State. The one object is to assert the supreme majesty of God, and this is also the theme of the next words, in which God is described under the 16 three attributes which set Him apart from all created beings. He is eternal, transcendent, invisible. While He sustains the world He is yet above it, and man's attitude towards Him can only be one of boundless awe. **To Him be honour and eternal power ; Amen.**

This doxology, borrowed perhaps from some Jewish or Christian liturgy, is not thrown in conventionally, to bring the Epistle to a dignified close. By means of it the writer gives definite expression to the two ideas which underlie his thought all through these letters : (1) The ultimate interest of the Church is a religious one. There must be right organization and a high moral standard, social and individual, but everything else must rest on faith in God. Nothing can be further from the truth than to conceive of the Pastorals as a mere ecclesiastical handbook in which the deeper religious motive is almost wanting. (2) As the Church stands for religion, so it must hold to the true religion as against all perversions. The writer lives in a time when gnostic teachers were playing fast and loose with the conception of God; he feels that before the Christian life is possible men must be sure in their minds of what they mean by God. Everything must be rooted in such a conception of the Divine nature as is set forth in the doxology.

WARNING TO THE RICH (vi. 17–19)

17 Charge the rich of this world not to be supercilious, and not
to fix their hopes on so uncertain a thing as riches but on
the living God who richly provides us with all the joys of
18 life ; bid them be bountiful, rich in good works, open-
19 handed and generous, amassing right good[1] treasure for
themselves in the world to come, so as to secure the life
which is life indeed.

These verses may seem to come in strangely between the
lofty doxology and the final benediction. It has been held by
some critics that they were inserted by a later hand, or that
they stood originally after verse 2. But the apparent awk-
wardness is due to the long parenthesis comprised in verses
11–16. In verses 6–10 the writer began to deal with the
subject of riches, but held this theme in suspense while he
contrasted the life devoted to material things with the true
and everlasting life. Now he returns to his main subject, and
as he has spoken before to those who are seeking for riches he
proceeds to offer a warning to those who are already rich.
With his usual moderation he does not denounce them or bid
them surrender everything. He only tells them that in their
worldly prosperity they must not forget God, and that they
must use what He has given them to a right purpose. The
language strongly recalls some of the sayings in the Gospels
(e.g. Matt. vi. 19 ; Luke xii. 16–21 ; xvi. 9), and it is more
than likely that the writer had these words of Jesus in his
mind.

17 Charge the rich of this world not to be supercilious (lit.
' not to think loftily '), conceiving themselves to be quite
secure from the changes and perils to which other men are
subject ; and not to fix their hopes on so uncertain a thing as
riches. The parable of the man who built his house on the
sand may lie behind this warning. Wealth appears to most

---

[1] For Θεμέλιον I accept the attractive conjecture Θέμα λίαν, in view of the
close parallel in Tobit iv. 9–10 (Θέμα γὰρ ἀγαθὸν Θησαυρίζεις σεαυτῷ εἰς ἡμέραν
ἀνάγκης. διότι Ἐλεημοσύνη ἐκ Θανάτου ῥύεται).

men to be the one thing they can count upon in this unstable world, but nothing is so uncertain. If we would be free from all anxiety, our hopes must be based **on the living God, who richly provides us with all the joys of life.** The suggestion is that we ought to look away from mere possessions to God, the living source of all good ; so long as we are sure of Him we have access to a wealth that can never fail us. At the same time the thought of iv. 4, 5 is taken up again. Earthly good things are given by God, who means them to be enjoyed. The ascetic attitude to this world as intrinsically evil is again condemned. Nothing is demanded of rich men except that, while availing themselves of their possessions, they should use **18** them in order to be **bountiful, rich in good works, open-handed and generous** (lit. ' ready to share '). Of these two last words the former describes merely the act of liberal giving ; the other lays stress on the human sympathy which ought to accompany the gift. **Amassing right good treasure for them- 19 selves in the world to come.** The text reads ' a good foundation,' which Moffatt emends, as he explains in a footnote, on the ground of a striking parallel in the book of Tobit. ' Storing up or laying up in store a good foundation ' is admittedly a strange metaphor, but the emendation also has its difficulties. It not only involves a very unusual word for ' treasure,' but it qualifies this word in a manner which would be next to impossible in Greek. Perhaps the language of the verse is best explained when we assume that the parable of the two houses is floating before the writer's mind. He has thought of the one man who built on the shifting sand, and this suggests to him the other man who ' laid a foundation ' (Luke vi. 48). It is possible, too, that he plays on the double meaning of the Greek word, which can signify a ' fund ' as well as a ' foundation.' In any case the general sense is clear, and is brought out in Moffatt's rendering. Wealth is in itself uncertain, but by a proper use of it men can obtain something firm and enduring, so that by giving away they are in reality laying up for the future. **For themselves** is emphatic. By sharing with others you not only help those who are in need, but gain for your own soul what is far more valuable than anything you give. The thought thus conveyed by a metaphor is clearly stated in the next words, **so as to secure the life that is life indeed.** The whole passage 6–19 has turned on the contrast between the material life which finds its satisfaction in riches, and the true life on which the Christian must set his heart. This true life will be given hereafter in all its fulness, but it can be achieved even now, and is the only life which is worthy of the name.

FINAL ADMONITION (vi. 20–21)

20 O Timotheus, keep the securities of the faith intact; avoid the profane jargon and contradictions of what is falsely
21   called ' Knowledge.' Certain individuals have failed in the faith by professing that. Grace be with you. Amen.

The Epistle closes with two verses which bring to a point all that has been said as to the need of preserving the gospel
20 in its purity. **Keep the securities of the faith intact** (lit. ' guard the deposit '). This word is found again in 2 Tim. i. 12 and i. 14, while there are repeated allusions to a trust which has been handed down and must be guarded faithfully. This ' deposit ' in the widest sense includes the whole of Christianity as it has come down from Christ through the apostles. Timothy, as Paul's successor, is to see to it that the Christian rule of life is observed, that the Church is wisely governed and purged from all base elements. In the present passage it is mainly this matter of doctrine which is in question; but doctrine and practice are closely connected for this writer. False teaching is condemned because it is the prime source of error in Christian living. Timothy is therefore to **avoid the profane jargon.** This word ' profane ' has been used already (iv. 7), and denotes that which is common, in contrast to that which is sacred. Thus it is applied to persons whose interests are wholly material (Heb. xii. 16), and here (as in 2 Tim. ii. 16) to modes of teaching which are foreign to religion although they affect religious language. They are also described as ' empty sounds,' no doubt with reference to the jargon which played a great part in gnosticism, as in all sham philosophies

since. The strange terms were impressive and seemed to mean much, but were found, when you examined them, to be only empty sounds. They are further described as **contradictions of what is falsely called 'Knowledge.'** Here, perhaps, we have the clearest indication given us in the Epistles that the false teaching was of a gnostic type. Its exponents laid claim to a ' gnosis ' or higher knowledge, although, in the writer's view, they were misusing a great word. A theory has been advanced that the verse contains a direct reference not only to gnosis but to a notorious gnostic book, the *Antitheses* of the heretic Marcion. The book is now lost, but dealt, apparently, with the ' contradictions ' between the Law (assigned to an inferior God) and the gospel. This work of Marcion, however, must be dated considerably later than our Epistles. According to another view there is an allusion to the Jewish practice of putting the opinions of rival rabbis over against each other, a practice which may also be indicated in the reference to ' legal contentions ' in Titus i. 9. But there is no reason to suppose that the writer has any specific book or practice in his mind. He is simply following up his description of the false teaching as ' empty talk.' It is said to consist in **contradictions** because the heretics aimed at nothing but to oppose the true beliefs which had come down from the apostles. By 21 **professing this false knowledge**—flaunting it as a higher truth —some **have failed in the faith** (lit. ' have missed the mark '). The same word was used at the beginning of the Epistle, and in its repetition at the very end we have a clue to the writer's main purpose. He is aware of the mischief wrought by current perversions of the gospel, and seeks to bring the Church back to the genuine tradition, which for him was enshrined in the teaching and example of Paul. After the Pauline manner the Epistle closes with a benediction : **Grace be with you.** It is significant that the plural is used, although the letter purports to be written to Timothy alone. Perhaps the writer forgets the supposed setting of the letter, and simply takes over a familiar Pauline formula. More likely he wishes to indicate that the counsels addressed to Timothy have a value for all Christian teachers and for the Church at large.

THE SECOND EPISTLE OF PAUL TO TIMOTHEUS

THE SECOND EPISTLE OF PAUL TO TIMOTHEUS

i.

Paul an apostle of Christ Jesus by the will of God, in the service 1
of the Life He has promised in Christ Jesus—to his beloved 2
son Timotheus ; grace, mercy, peace, from God the Father
and Christ Jesus our Lord.

The salutation follows the model which is customary in
ancient letters, and which may be traced in the opening of all
the Epistles of Paul : ' A to B sends greeting.' Paul, however,
invariably expands this formula in a Christian sense, and here
it is further modified in such a manner as to strike at once the
two dominant notes of the Epistle : (*a*) the personal affection
of Paul for Timothy ; (*b*) the choice of Timothy as the successor to whom he bequeathes his mission and authority.

Paul an apostle of Christ Jesus by the will of God. This 1
designation is elsewhere meant to vindicate Paul's apostleship,
which had been challenged by his Jewish opponents. Its
purpose here is to impress on Timothy the nature of the trust
which is now to be laid on him. He is to maintain the Christian
tradition in the name of Paul, the divinely appointed apostle.
The trust had been conferred on Paul himself **in the service of**
the Life promised in Christ Jesus (lit. ' according to a promise
of life '). Paul has the right to call himself an apostle in so far
as he makes known this promise. His message, in the last
resort, consists in nothing else than in assuring men that in
Christ they will find eternal life. **To his beloved son Timotheus.** 2
The terms of endearment are to be understood in something
like a literal sense. As Paul's own convert, Timothy was
spiritually his son, and of all his spiritual children Paul loves
him the best. In an ordinary letter the greeting would consist
of the single word ' joy,' but this is replaced by a kindred word
which means ' grace ' or ' favour,' and is expanded into a

benediction. This christianizing of the ordinary terms of courtesy is characteristic of all Paul's letters.

THANKSGIVING (i. 3–5)

3 I render thanks to God, the God of my fathers whom I worship with a pure conscience, as I mention you constantly in
4 my prayers. When I recall the tears you shed when we
5 parted, I long by night and day to see you again ; that would fill me with joy, for I am reminded of your sincere faith, a faith which dwelt first in your grandmother Lois and your mother Eunice, as it dwells (I am certain) in yourself.

In letters of the time the opening salutation was followed by a few words of pious thanks for the health and prosperity of the person addressed. The custom is likewise observed in Paul's Epistles, but the conventional phrases are changed into Christian ones, and are made to express a genuine feeling.

3 **I render thanks to God, the God of my fathers whom I worship** (lit. ' whom I worship from my ancestors ') **with a pure conscience.** Two ideas are involved : (*a*) Paul belonged to a family which had always practised the worship of the true God ; (*b*) in his own person he had always been faithful to this worship. This might seem to conflict with the confession in 1 Tim. i. 13 that he had formerly been a blasphemer and persecutor ; but he was there speaking only of his attitude to the gospel. He can truly say, as he does here, that he had always been perfectly sincere in his service of God. As a Christian, Paul was thrown into bitter opposition to Judaism, but he never fails to speak of it with profound respect, and was proud of his Jewish antecedents (Rom. ix. 3–5; Phil. iii. 4–6). He mentions them here because he is going to congratulate Timothy on a similar advantage which he owed to his family traditions. This, indeed, appears to be the real object of his thanksgiving. The sentence is never properly finished, and runs off into a digression, but we can gather from what follows

that his purpose is to thank God that Timothy has been worthy of the family from which he sprang. **As I mention you constantly in my prayers**—i.e. while praying for Timothy, as he continually does, he remembers certain facts about him. **When I recall the tears you shed when we parted, I long night 4 and day to see you again.** This is probably suggested by the moving incident in Acts xx. 37, when Paul's Ephesian friends broke into tears as they said farewell to him at Miletus. It is implied that Timothy had been one of the company, and that Paul and he had been separated during the six years or more which had since elapsed. Paul had been longing for him all the time—**for I am reminded of your sincere faith.** The word **faith** is here used in the general sense of religious feeling. This is indicated by the adjective which describes it, **for the** question of sincerity cannot arise in that inner relation of the soul to God which Paul usually defines as Faith. It is further 5 indicated by the comparison of Timothy's faith **to that which dwelt first in your grandmother Lois and your mother Eunice.** The meaning may be that Timothy's grandmother had been the first of his family to become a Christian, and that her conversion had led to that of his mother, and finally of himself. This would imply that she had been **converted in her old age,** when Paul, on his first missionary journey, had brought the message to Lystra ; but it is more natural to explain the words in the broader sense that she had been a notably pious woman. Just as Paul's own family had been faithful to their religion for generations, so had the family of Timothy. His father, as we know from Acts xvi. 1, was a Greek, but on his mother's side he came of a devout Jewish stock. By the word **first** it is not meant that the religious strain only began to show itself in his grandmother, but only that he had been subject to religious influences as far back as he could remember. This notice of Timothy's family is probably genuine, for even if the Epistle is not by Paul it yet dates from a time when memories of Timothy were still current in the Church. It was known that his mother and grandmother had been conspicuously pious women, and this piety, the sentence concludes, **dwells (I am certain, I feel sure) in yourself.** His upbringing by such holy women was a guarantee that his own religion was genuine and had come to him as a birthright.

ENCOURAGEMENT TO FRESH EFFORT (i. 6–12)

6 Hence I would remind you to rekindle the divine gift which
7   you received when my hands were laid upon you ; for God
    has not given us a timid spirit but a spirit of power and love
8   and discipline. So do not be ashamed to testify to our
    Lord, and do not be ashamed of a prisoner of the Lord like
    myself ; join me in bearing suffering for the gospel by the
9   power of the God who has saved us and called us to a life of
    consecration—not for anything we have done but because
    He chose to do it Himself, by the grace which He gave us
10   ages ago in Christ Jesus and has now revealed in the
    appearance of our Saviour Jesus Christ, who has put down
    death and brought life and immortality to light by the
11   gospel. Of that gospel I have been appointed a herald
12   and an apostle and a teacher, and this is why I suffer as
    I do. Still, I am not ashamed of it ; I know whom I have
    trusted, and I am certain that He is able to keep what I have
    put into His hands till the great Day.

It is impressed on Timothy that he has three motives to exert himself even more strenuously in his work : (1) the sense of a Divine commission with which he was entrusted at his ordination ; (2) the example of Paul's own labour and suffering ; (3) the knowledge of a new life which has been given to men through Christ. The rest of the Epistle may be regarded as the amplification and enforcement of these three motives.

6   Hence—i.e. because I have full confidence in your genuine religious spirit—I would remind you to rekindle the divine gift. Some have here found a suggestion that Timothy had allowed himself to weaken in his Christian zeal ; but there is no hint of this in the body of the Epistle. The idea is rather that something already aglow should be fanned into flame. Timothy had received a true spiritual gift, and the duty is

thereby laid on him to make it fully effective by earnest Christian service. The gift was bestowed **when my hands were laid upon you.** The reference cannot be to baptism, for the ' gift,' as the sequel shows, is the specific one of leadership in the Church, and this was conferred by ordination. It is assumed that the ceremony, while itself an outward one, carried with it a Divine sanction ; the official appointment was at the same time an investiture with power from God. Here we find the beginning of the later Catholic doctrine of ordination as a ' sacrament,' but behind the doctrine there was an idea inherited from the Primitive Church. In setting apart certain men for active work in the mission the Church was supposed to act on the impulse of the Spirit (Acts xiii. 1) ; but in this earlier conception the emphasis was laid on the choice of the Spirit, while in the later one it was placed on the ceremony itself. In 1 Tim. iv. 14, Timothy is said to have been ordained by the board of presbyters, and there is mention here of Paul alone. But there is no contradiction. Paul does not speak of the elders who concurred with him, because he is leading up to the idea which he intends to be the main one; he had designed that Timothy should be his successor, and, by laying his hands on him, he had transmitted his own function and authority. **For God has not given us a timid spirit** (lit. ' a 7 spirit of timidity '). The idea of a spiritual gift here blends with that of the Spirit itself. All Christians were supposed to receive the Spirit, but the one Spirit (according to 1 Cor. xii. 1f.) produced different activities in different men. As it was given to us—i.e. to Christian leaders such as Paul and Timothy —it was not one that entailed timidity. The writer may be thinking of Christians who undoubtedly are finely gifted with the Spirit, but for that very reason are nervous and shrinking. Our own poet Cowper is a well-known example. It is not in this manner, however, that the Spirit works in an active apostle. He receives **a spirit of power** enabling him to face difficulty boldly and exercise authority ; **a spirit of love,** in the sense not merely of affection but of practical helpfulness ; **a spirit of discipline**—i.e. a capacity to influence and direct one's fellow-men. (In its substantive form the word occurs only

I<small>E</small>   91

here, although the verb is used in Titus ii. 4 of the control which the older women are to exercise over the younger.)

8 **So do not be ashamed to testify to our Lord.** Here, as throughout the passage, we have an echo of the language of Paul, but a different turn is given to the borrowed phrase. Paul had said, in Rom. i. 16, ' I am not ashamed of the gospel of Christ.' This now becomes ' do not be ashamed to bear witness to Christ,' and the reason why shame might be felt is suggested in the next words, ' nor of me his prisoner.' The Christian missionary was enlisted in a suffering cause, and had to acknowledge as his friends men who were in prison, under social disgrace. As in Eph. iii. 1 and Phil. i. 12, Paul is made to describe himself as Christ's **prisoner**, not merely in the sense that men have imprisoned him as a follower of Christ ; the thought is rather that Christ Himself has made him a prisoner for some hidden purpose of His own. **Join me in bearing suffering for the gospel.** Instead of feeling shame for Paul, Timothy is to hold himself prepared to suffer likewise. The reference may be general ('accept hardship as I have done '), but in Heb. xiii. 23 we learn that Timothy, perhaps twenty years after Paul's death, had lately been freed from prison. There may here be an allusion to that experience of Timothy, which was literally to repeat that of Paul. He is assured that if he suffers it will be ' according to **the power of God** ' ; strength will be given him in proportion to what he must endure. The strength

9 will be more than sufficient since it comes from God, **who has saved us and called us to a life of consecration** (lit. ' by a holy calling '). God has not only effected the Christian salvation, but has enabled us to receive it, calling individually each one of His elect. He calls us **not for anything we have done** ' but according to His own purpose and grace.' The certainty of the call is thus ensured. If it depended on our own deserving, we might well feel doubtful, but it has its ground in God's own will, which cannot be shaken. This is the real motive in Paul's doctrine of predestination, which has so often been misunderstood ; Paul is anxious to put the Christian salvation on a basis absolutely secure. Men are to feel, in spite of their fear and weakness, that they can rely on God's mercy, which is quite

irrespective of any fault or merit of their own. God Himself gave the salvation in Christ Jesus, ages ago. This same phrase ages ago is used in Titus i. 2 to denote the remote antiquity of the Old Testament promises. Here it echoes the thought of Eph. i. 4, that God had called His people from all eternity. The grace had been given before the world was made, but has now been revealed in the appearance of our Saviour Christ Jesus. Behind these words there is the thought of something which had already taken place in that higher world which is hidden from us. What happened on earth was only the manifestation in space and time of the things of eternity. The writer has rightly grasped Paul's idea of the act of salvation as bound up with a cosmic drama, the meaning of which was disclosed by the appearance of Christ. This word, applied in I Tim. vi. 14 to the return of Christ in glory, is here used of His earthly coming. In Hellenistic religion it denoted the birthday of the god, or the action in which he pre-eminently displayed himself in his divine character. This meaning is preserved in the name given to the feast of the ' Epiphany '—i.e. the Baptism—when Jesus was declared to be the Son of God. The name Saviour which is applied to Christ was also taken over, at least in its specific sense, from Hellenistic religion, so that two words of a similar origin are here brought into close connexion. From this it has sometimes been inferred that the teaching of the Pastorals is affiliated in some special way to that of the mystery cults, but the very opposite is true. There is practically nothing in these Epistles of the mysticism which was characteristic of the cults, and which reflects itself in the thought of Paul and John. All that can be concluded is that when the Epistles were written Christianity had become definitely a Gentile religion, and was freely borrowing ideas and terms from its pagan surroundings.

Christ, then, has been described as Saviour, and the next words explain why the name may be justly given to Him. He has put down death and brought life and immortality to light by the gospel. According to Paul, Christ by His death had destroyed the power of death, and by His resurrection had entered on the new life which His people now share with Him.

In the present passage nothing is said of the manner in which death has been overcome. The whole stress is laid on the fact itself. Christ is the Saviour because men have received through Him the knowledge of a future life. It might almost appear as if the writer shared the gnostic view that the true work of Christ had consisted in imparting to His disciples a marvellous revelation as to the nature and origin of the soul, and the secrets of the higher world. This, however, is not the meaning. The gospel as it is here conceived is the announcement of all that Christ had done and taught. He had manifested the Divine life, and the idea of this manifestation is blended with that of the gospel which tells about it. The knowledge given thus through the gospel is described by a peculiar word, brought to light. This is yet another term which was taken over by the Church from the mystery religions, in which it denoted the illumination of the initiate by means of secret rites. Probably, to begin with, the word was something more than a metaphor. In the course of his initiation, as we know from several ancient sources, the votary was led out of a dark chamber into a sudden blaze of light, and in this moment was supposed to be born again into a new life. The word ' enlighten ' was adopted by the Church as a regular term for conversion or baptism, and is so found in the Epistle to Hebrews (vi. 4, x. 32). It is applied in the present passage not to the person ' enlightened,' but to the truth in which the light consisted ; although it suggests, at the same time, that those who receive this truth have been transformed. Christ has brought light to them in the knowledge of ' life and incorruption '—i.e. a life which is not subject to decay. By the power of this message men are lifted out of the sphere of the transient and material. They have part in the eternal life.

The passage is meant to summarize the main conceptions of the gospel as Paul had proclaimed it. But while he makes use of various Pauline texts, the writer betrays himself at every point as the representative of a later type of teaching. The effects which Paul himself ascribes to the death of Christ are made to depend on the whole appearance, on the Incarnation rather than on the Cross. The gospel is regarded as itself a

Divine agency; in other words, nothing is required of the Christian but to put his faith in the approved doctrines, and by doing so he will obtain the new life. Even in his language the writer mixes the Pauline terms with others, which belong to the Hellenized theology of the later Church.

The aim of the passage is to state briefly the nature of the message which had found its true exponent in Paul, and the transition is now made to Paul himself, who is about to throw his mantle on Timothy his successor. **Of that gospel I have 11 been appointed a herald and an apostle and a teacher.** Reference was made in verse 8 to the ' witness ' which Paul had been called on to render, and the duty which had been laid on him is now more fully stated. Apostles, prophets, and teachers were three distinct orders of ministry in the Primitive Church, and attempts have been made to give separate meanings to the terms employed here. This, however, is unnecessary. The precise meaning of the three terms had now been forgotten, and they are thrown loosely together to enforce the idea that Paul had a unique authority as a teacher of the gospel. He had expounded it, under Divine guidance, in all its aspects, and there could be no genuine Christian teaching which was not in line with the Pauline tradition. All true and effective 12 witness entails suffering, and the apostle points to his sufferings as proof of his fidelity. In addition to all his previous hardships he had now been thrown into prison; if Timothy might be ashamed of such an associate, the prisoner himself might well be more so. But he is content to suffer, ' **for I know whom I have trusted.**' Who is it in whom the apostle has this absolute confidence ? We naturally think of Christ, but the previous passage has been concerned with the power of God, and it is the same power which is now in question. ' **I am certain that He, who has all other power, is able to keep what I have put into His hands** [lit. to guard my deposit], **till the great Day.**' The image is that of something precious which has been left in trusty hands for safe keeping ; and the same word ' deposit ' is repeated five times in 1 and 2 Timothy. In all the other passages it clearly has reference to the Christian faith which has been committed to Paul and Timothy as its guardians.

Here it might seem to denote something which Paul has entrusted to God, and for this reason he declares that he is sure of God ; he knows that God has both the power and the will to guard what has been committed to Him. None the less, the ' deposit ' is best explained, as in the other passages, in the sense of the Christian message with which Paul himself has been entrusted. We should naturally expect him to say that he is fully conscious of his responsibility, and has resolved that nothing will ever tempt him to be false to his great commission. This, in effect, is what he says ; but he remembers the uncertainty of all human resolves. He therefore calls on God to take the precious ' deposit ' under His own protection. He has confidence in himself because he can rely on God. In this way the image of a deposit may almost be understood literally. The man entrusted with a valuable jewel or document is careful to have it placed in some strong room where it will be guarded night and day. He is nervous and anxious until it has passed out of his own doubtful keeping into one that he can depend on. Paul thus conceives of the trust that has been laid upon him as guarded for him by God. The verse has usually been explained as similar in meaning to I Pet. iv. 19, where those who suffer are exhorted ' to commit their souls to God as to a faithful Creator ' ; Paul would thus assure himself that he is safe amidst all dangers since he has entrusted his true life to God, who will give it back to him on that great Day. This meaning, however, is foreign to the whole tenor of the passage, as well as to the author's constant idea of the ' deposit.' Only one interpretation fits in with all the requirements. Paul, as the guardian of Christian truth, is conscious of his solemn obligation and also of his own inadequacy. He calls on God Himself to safeguard the message which He has given. Perhaps the mention of ' that day ' points to a reminiscence of the parable of the Talents. A charge has been committed to Paul as to the stewards in the parable, and he is confident that on the day of account he will not be found wanting.

PAUL'S EXAMPLE AN ENCOURAGEMENT TO TIMOTHY (i. 13-14)

Model yourself on the sound instruction you have had from me 13
 in the faith and love of Christ Jesus. Keep the great 14
 securities of your faith intact, by aid of the holy Spirit that
 dwells within us.

As Paul's successor Timothy is to keep his example ever
before him. **Model yourself on the sound instruction** is literally 13
' As an outline of healthy words retain those which you heard
from me.' A peculiar word is used which does not mean so
much a pattern as a sketch or ground-plan. Timothy is not
told to repeat just the things which Paul had said. All that is
required of him is to keep Paul's teaching before his mind, as an
architect designs a building on the general plan of some other
which has proved suitable for its purpose. As constantly in
these Epistles, the right doctrine is described as **sound** or
' healthy,' free from all infection of error ; and Timothy is
to hold it **in the faith and love of Christ Jesus,** faith and love
here forming a single concept for the loyal affection which
marks the servant of Christ. The object of the words is to
ensure that Timothy should not cling formally to a given
creed ; Paul has supplied the doctrine, but Timothy must
bring to it the sympathy and understanding by which he can
make it his own. He is to ' guard the precious deposit ' which
Paul himself has guarded, and which has been given him in
that ' healthy teaching ' to which his own must conform. He
will thus take up and hand down to others the message with
which Paul had been entrusted. And as Paul had relied on a 14
Divine power to keep him faithful, so Timothy may count on
the **aid of the holy Spirit that dwells in us.** The thought of
verse 6 is here repeated—that a special gift has been bestowed
on Timothy as on all true Christian leaders. In the earlier
time the Spirit was regarded as the possession of all Christians,
and this is what Paul means, in other Epistles, when he speaks
of ' the Spirit which dwells in us ' (cf. Rom. viii. 9). But we
have now an anticipation of the later doctrine for which the
Spirit was the special endowment of the Church's ministry.

The idea, which was meant originally to affirm the liberty of all believers, was now used to enforce the authority of the ordained officers.

CONCRETE INSTANCES OF PERVERSION AND FIDELITY

(i. 15–18)

15 You are aware that all the Asiatics have discarded me, including
16   Phygelus and Hermogenes. May the Lord show favour
    to the household of Onesiphorus, for many a time he braced
17   me up ; he was not ashamed of my imprisonment—no, he
    made eager search for me when he reached Rome, and he
    found me (may he find favour with the Lord on the great
18   Day ! The Lord grant it !). And you know right well what
    a help he was to me in Ephesus.

Timothy has been exhorted to keep faithful to Paul's example. He is now reminded of men known to him who
15 serve to illustrate the warning. You are aware that all (in Asia) the Asiatics have discarded me, including Phygelus and Hermogenes. By ' Asia ' is meant the Roman province of that name, of which Ephesus was the capital. The ' turning away ' does not imply apostasy from the faith, for it is contrasted with the personal loyalty of Onesiphorus ; evidently the meaning is that Paul had met with indifference and coldness from friends who ought to have stood by him. Fear has been expressed that Timothy might become ashamed of his old master, now that he was a prisoner, and examples are given to show that this fear was not imaginary. It would be natural to suppose that the incidents mentioned had taken place in Rome, where Asiatic Christians who might have befriended Paul had stood aloof. Strictly taken, however, the words would imply disloyalty of ' those in Asia.' Perhaps Paul had written to Ephesus, asking that some of his old friends should come to his assistance at his approaching trial, and no one had volunteered. For some reason he was particularly hurt by the conduct of Phygelus and Hermogenes, two men of whom nothing is known. In contrast to them he dwells on the kindness he had received

from Onesiphorus, who is mentioned again in the final greet- 16 ings (iv. 19). In that later reference, as here, Paul offers his gratitude to **the household of Onesiphorus,** suggesting that the man himself was now dead. **Many a time he braced me up** (lit. ' refreshed me '). It does not appear that Onesiphorus had helped him with gifts, or even with active support. What he remembers with gratitude is simply the evidence which this friend had given, by his frequent visits, that **he was not ashamed of my imprisonment.** The literal word is ' my chain,' and this graphic touch gives point to the allusion. While awaiting trial, Paul was allowed to live in his own quarters and hold intercourse with his friends (Acts xxviii. 30) ; but in this *custodia libera et honesta* he had still to bear the mark of degradation, attached as he was by a light chain to a soldier who was always on guard. **He made eager search for me when** 17 **he reached Rome.** Onesiphorus had come to Rome, as the language implies, on his own business, and to discover Paul's obscure lodging in the huge unknown city was a matter of great difficulty. Only a true friend would have put himself to the trouble. **May he find favour with the Lord on the great Day !** 18 **The Lord grant it !** The name **Lord** may here be applied first to Christ and then to God ; but more likely the prayer is addressed in both clauses to God. Sometimes the verse has been adduced as scriptural support for the custom of prayer for the dead. It is to be noted, however, that the prayer has reference to the future judgment, and is only the expression of a very natural feeling. As he thinks of this good friend, Paul is convinced that God in the end will reward him. Possibly the idea of finding **favour** is suggested by the previous phrase **he found me.** One who made search for a friend in trouble had a right to succeed in the great quest for favour in the sight of God. **And you know right well what a help he was to me in Ephesus.** The literal words are, ' you know better than I '; and the allusion may be to some action which Onesiphorus had taken in Ephesus without Paul's knowledge, or after his departure. The final charity in Rome had been only the climax of a consistent loyalty.

99

RENEWED ENCOURAGEMENT TO BRAVE SERVICE (ii. 1-7)

ii.

1-2 Now, my son, be strong in the grace of Christ Jesus, and, as for the instructions I gave you in presence of many witnesses, transmit them to trustworthy men, that they may be competent to teach others.

3 Join the ranks of those who bear suffering, like a loyal soldier
4 of Christ Jesus. No soldier gets entangled in civil pursuits ;
5 his aim is to satisfy his commander. Again, a competitor in the games is not crowned unless he observes the rules.
6 The farmer who has done the work must have the first
7 share of the fruit. Think what I mean ! The Lord will help you to understand it perfectly.

1 **Now, my son** (the Greek is emphatic, ' For your part,' in contrast to those who have failed in their duty), **be strong in the grace of Christ Jesus.** He has spoken already of a power which has been divinely bestowed on Timothy (i. 6, 7). Conscious
2 of this power supporting him, Timothy is to put forth his utmost effort and **transmit the instructions I gave you in the presence of** (lit. ' through ') **many witnesses.** The preposition ' through ' is sometimes found in Greek with the sense ' in presence of,' and this may be the intention here. If so, the reference is to some solemn occasion, such as ordination, when Paul had impressed on Timothy the cardinal Christian beliefs and duties. Many had been present when the charge was given, and can testify against Timothy if he fails to act on it or interprets it wrongly. But the appeal has more significance when we take ' through ' in its natural sense. Paul is reminding Timothy of the fundamental Christian truths which must be faithfully handed down. Timothy had heard them from Paul, but since Paul himself had received them under the attestation of many others, including the personal disciples of Jesus, they may be accepted with full confidence as the primary demands, acknowledged by all who from the beginning had held the Christian faith. Timothy, in his turn, is to impart them **to trustworthy men, that they may be competent to teach others.** The genuine Christian teaching is

a divine treasure which Paul had guarded faithfully, and he now places it in the hands of Timothy, who must convey it to others, so that it may be passed on to future times ; it is of inestimable value to the human race, and must be preserved and handed down without injury. We have here the earliest hint of an apostolic succession, but at a later time the stress was laid on certain qualifications which were passed on from one body of officers to the next. Here it is the ' deposit ' itself which is in question. The men are important only as custodians of the treasure, and all that is required of them is fidelity in their trust ; for this reason it is imperative that they should be rightly instructed, and that they should be themselves men of the highest character. This, as the writer conceives it, is the true apostolic succession, a series of men who will carry on the work of the apostles with the same faith and sincerity.

Join the ranks of those who bear suffering, like a loyal 3 soldier of Christ Jesus. In i. 8 Timothy was called on to suffer along with Paul, and the idea is now made general. The Christian service entails suffering, and must be accepted on that condition. Paul had already pictured the Christian as a soldier, clothed in full armour (Eph. vi. 10f.), and in the second century the term ' soldier of Christ ' had become almost another name for ' Christian.' The idea implied in it was primarily that of aiding Christ in His warfare on the forces of evil ; perhaps it owed something to the Persian conception of a struggle between the mysterious principles of good and evil, in which all men were required to bear their part. In the Pastorals the object of the warfare almost falls out of sight ; attention is concentrated on the discipline imposed on the Christian, who must be prepared, like a good soldier, to endure every hardship. The Christian teacher is pre-eminently a soldier, and as such he must devote himself entirely to his military duties. **No soldier** (lit. ' no man on 4 active service ') **gets entangled in civil pursuits.** The Christian is not merely a soldier, but is in the fighting line, and must hold aloof from all occupations which may be right enough in themselves but are not directly concerned with his service.

His aim is to satisfy his commander; there must be no thought in a soldier's mind except to carry out his orders, and the Christian must be content to obey, regardless of his own profit and inclination. The comparison with the soldier is followed by two others, one with an athlete, the second with a farmer. All three are commonly employed in the literature of the time, and have found their way from ancient ethical thought into our own—e.g. 'fighting a temptation,' 'wrestling with a difficulty,' 'cultivating a character.' It can hardly be accidental that the language of the present passage closely resembles that in which Paul himself speaks of the missionary life. 'Who goes a warfare at his own charges? Who plants a vineyard and eats not of the fruits?' (I Cor. ix. 7). The metaphor of athletic training, also frequent in Paul—e.g. I Cor. ix. 24f.; Gal. v. 7; Phil. iii. 14—is here used to 5 strengthen the idea of good soldiership. But even a **competitor in the games** (one who engages in a mimic warfare instead of a real one) **is not crowned unless he observes the rules.** The meaning is not that he is disqualified if he breaks the rules of the game. As the context shows, it is the preparation for the contest which is in question and not the contest itself. An athlete has no chance of victory unless he has complied with certain previous conditions; he must have undergone the necessary training and limited himself to a given diet. Like the soldier he must give up everything with the one object 6 of winning the game. The next metaphor is to the same effect. **The farmer who has done the work must have the first share of the fruit.** As the athlete aims at a crown, so the farmer seeks to produce a crop, and he who has worked hardest has the first right to the fruits of his labour. In this case the illustration is far-fetched, and has probably been thrown in because it occurs in I Cor. ix. 10f., a passage which the writer has before him throughout. In that passage Paul is concerned with the support to which missionaries are duly entitled, and the parallel with the farmer is an apt one: the theme here is entirely different. All three metaphors are intended to bring out the same idea—that the Christian teacher must devote himself wholly to his work, giving up all interests that might distract him. In all three, too, there is the added thought of a reward which is bestowed on the faithful worker. 7

Some words are appended to underline the importance of what has been said. **Think what I mean! The Lord will help you to understand it perfectly** (lit. 'will give you intelligence in all things '). The warnings have been expressed figuratively; but Timothy is to ' consider ' what they imply. Perhaps it is suggested that they may be difficult to carry out to their full extent. A Christian teacher, like other men, has worldly concerns from which he cannot shake himself quite free, but he must use his common sense and modify the rule when necessary. The important thing is to obey the spirit of the instructions, although they may be altered now and then in points of detail.

CHRIST AS THE MOTIVE TO CHRISTIAN SERVICE (ii. 8–13)

Never forget ' Jesus Christ risen from the dead, descended from 8
    David '—according to my gospel, for which I have to 9
    suffer imprisonment as if I were a criminal. (But there
    is no prison for the word of God.) All I endure is for the 10
    sake of the elect, to let them obtain their share of the
    salvation of Christ Jesus and also of eternal glory. It is a 11
    sure word, that

        ' If we have died with Him, we shall live with Him,
        if we endure, then we shall reign with Him, if we 12
        disown Him, then He will disown us,
        if we are faithless, He remains faithful '— 13

    for He cannot be untrue to Himself.

It was impressed on Timothy in the opening of the chapter that he would grow strong by the grace of Christ. The writer now returns to this theme of Christ Himself as the one inspiration of all Christian service. **Never forget ' Jesus Christ risen from the dead, descended from David.'** It is difficult to see why these two facts about Jesus are singled out and coupled together. Perhaps the intention is to drive home the idea that, although Christ is now exalted, He had shared our human life and therefore stands as our example. More likely the writer is simply following Rom. i. 3, 4, and mentions the descent of Jesus and His rising from the dead by way of solemn designation, as the dignities of a monarch are placed after his name. For primitive Christianity the descent from David was all-important, as the guarantee that Jesus was the Messiah foretold in prophecy. To Paul it had become a matter of indifference, and he alludes to it at the beginning of Romans only in deference to the settled belief. The added words, **according to my gospel,** also echo the language of Paul (Rom. ii. 16 ; xvi. 25) ; if they are meant to carry any special significance, it is that Timothy must keep true to the Pauline teaching with regard to the nature of Christ, avoiding the gnostic error that Christ had not truly died, and that He was 9 in some way distinct from the man Jesus. **For which I have to suffer imprisonment** (lit. ' I suffer hardship unto bonds '). Paul says that after all his other sufferings in the cause of the gospel he is now actually in ' bonds,' as if he **were a criminal.** Perhaps the meaning is more definite. Not only is he treated as any criminal might be, but, in the eyes of the law, he ranks as a criminal. We may here have an authentic notice of the charge on which Paul was tried and condemned. He was indicted, not as the teacher of a strange religion, but as a bandit or incendiary, whose presence, wherever he went, had been the signal for riot. Or perhaps the writer is thinking of Paul's martyrdom from the point of view of his own time. Towards the end of the first century the profession of Christianity became in itself a crime. Apart from any civic offence that might be urged against him, a Christian could be punished for the *nomen ipsum*, the mere fact that he called himself a Christian. This later position seems to be implied in the statement that Paul was suffering bonds for the gospel ; since he was a Christian teacher, the law regarded him as a criminal. **But there is no prison for the word of God** (lit. ' the word of God has not been bound '). Paul tells us, in

Phil. i. 13, that even in prison he had been able to do some work for the gospel. The words here, however, can hardly refer to those restricted activities which were still open to him, and the true meaning is well brought out in our translation. A contrast is drawn between the confinement which men can impose on the messenger and the liberty of the message. Since it is God's word, men can do nothing to hinder it. **All I endure is for the sake of the elect.** It was 10 Paul's belief that among the mass of men there were those who had been chosen by God to receive salvation. These elect souls were scattered throughout the world, and the object of the mission was to bring them the knowledge of the gospel, to which they would at once respond. So in this passage the thought is not so much of those already converted as of all the potential Christians who have not yet been reached. Since the message is free, it will work on, although the missionary has been bound ; it will in some way use his sufferings for its own purpose, **to let them also obtain their share of the salvation of Christ Jesus.** The whole passage turns on the thought that by Paul's suffering the gospel will extend itself more widely. Elsewhere he speaks of earthly suffering as ' working for us an eternal weight of glory ' (2 Cor. iv. 17). This has probably suggested the addition **and also of eternal glory** ; only, the idea is here applied to a glory which is won for others, not of the glory which will accrue to the Christian himself.

The passage closes with another of the ' faithful sayings.' 11 In this case there can be little doubt that the words quoted belong to a Christian hymn, for they are plainly of a rhythmical character, and almost set themselves to music. At the same time they are only part of the hymn, since the opening word ' for ' (' for if we be dead with Him ') must depend on something which has preceded. It is significant that the thought and even the language recall the passage on baptism in Rom. vi. 3f., and from this it may be inferred that the hymn was one which was sung on baptismal occasions, and would therefore be specially familar. The earlier part would deal, presumably, with the death and the risen life of Christ ; then with the call to put faith in Him as the Saviour. Thus the hymn would close with these words on the meaning of the faith expressed in baptism. ' For **if we have died with Him, we shall live with Him,**' is sometimes taken to refer to martyrdom ; but, in view of the parallel in Rom. vi. 4 ('we are buried with Him by baptism into death : that . . . we also should walk in newness of life '), it must be understood of the dying and rising with Christ which were symbolized in the baptismal rite. A symbolical death must be implied, since it 12 marks only the beginning of a life of self-denial. **If we endure, then we shall reign with Him**—i.e. we shall have part in His Kingdom when He returns to glory. The next sentence, **if we disown Him, He will disown us,** is plainly reminiscent of Luke ix. 26 (' whosoever shall be ashamed of Me and of My words, of him shall the Son of man be ashamed '), and would be specially appropriate if this is a baptismal hymn, sung over the convert who has just taken the oath of loyalty to 13 Christ. It has sometimes been held that the words which follow were added by the writer himself in order to correct or qualify the harsh statement that Christ will deny those who deny Him : **if we are faithless, He remains faithful.** But the words certainly belong to the hymn, and indeed constitute its chief beauty. Probably the very reason why the quotation is made is to bring in this magnificent assertion of the unchanging fidelity of Christ. The declaration in i. 9 that we are called ' not according to works, but according to His own purpose and grace ' is here transformed into poetry. There seems to be no good ground for holding (with Moffatt) that at least the closing words **for He cannot be untrue to Himself** are an addition of the writer's own. They are fully in the spirit of the poem, and are necessary to complete the thought of the verse before.

THE TEACHER AS A GUARDIAN OF RIGHT DOCTRINE (ii. 14–19)

14 Remind men of this : adjure them before the Lord not to
    bandy arguments—no good comes out of that, it only
15   means the undoing of your audience. Do your utmost

to let God see that you at least are a sound workman, with no need to be ashamed of the way that you handle the word of the Truth. Avoid all that profane jargon, for it 16 leads people still further into irreligion, and their doctrine 17 spreads like a gangrene. So it is with Hymenaeus and Philetus ; they have failed in the Truth by arguing that 18 the resurrection has taken place already, and they are undermining some people's faith. But the solid founda- 19 tion laid by God remains, and this is its inscription :

the Lord cares for His own,

and

' let everyone who names the name of the Lord give up evil.'

In the earlier part of the Epistle Timothy has been exhorted to keep before him the example of Paul. How he must follow it is now shown in detail. In the first place, Paul had stood for the genuine Christian teaching, and Timothy must see to it that the teaching is preserved, in face of rising heresies. ' Remind them of these things ' (i.e. of the primary truths of 14 the gospel as taught by Paul), ' and adjure them before the Lord not to bandy arguments.' Two interpretations can be given to the word here used, and our understanding of the verse that follows will depend on which of them we accept. It means literally ' word-fighting,' and may thus apply to controversy. Moffatt takes the word in this sense, and translates the verse as a counsel to Timothy not to waste his time in arguing with the false teachers. No good comes out of that ; it can have no other result than the undoing of your audience. The warning would thus be directed against the type of preacher who states false opinions with the object of refuting them, and succeeds only in awakening doubts which most of his hearers would never otherwise have thought of. The only teaching which can do good is positive, not controversial. There is much to commend this explanation of the verse, but two things are against it : (1) The ambiguous word occurs again in 1 Tim. vi. 4, where it distinctly refers to the verbal disputes, the 'empty talk' of the false teachers. (2) The solemn adjuration before the Lord must apply to something more serious than a well-meant but mistaken method of preaching. So it seems best to understand the verse in the light of the other meaning of the word. Here, as elsewhere, the writer takes the ground that the heretical speculations are mere trifling—'a strife about words.' He holds that they are mischievous because they distract men from the realities of the gospel to questions from which no good can come, and which serve only for 'the subversion of the hearers.' The word here used means just the opposite of Paul's favourite word 'edification.' Mere abstract questioning does not lead to any solid results. It does not build up, but only destroys faith by weakening the foundations. In this passage, therefore, the writer takes a characteristic attitude to the new teaching. Paul himself had recognized that vital interests were involved in it, and had put forth his utmost power in refuting the heretics at Colossae. This writer holds that all the dispute about abstract, speculative matters was only a 'fighting about words.' No doubt in some respects he was right. The heretical teachers had often little more than an intellectual interest in religion, and men to whom religion was intensely real could feel that they were not worth answering. Yet the questions they raised were by no means fanciful, and it was often the most sincere and thoughtful members of the Church to whom they appeared most important.

15   If Timothy is to check the inroads of false teaching, he will do so most effectually by showing in his own person what a true teacher ought to be. **Do your utmost to let God see that you are** (lit. ' to present yourself to God ') **a sound workman.** Timothy is to keep before him the thought of the Judgment, when he must give account to God for the manner in which he has performed his duty. There is a double emphasis on ' yourself ' **(you at least)** and on ' God.' Others may go astray, but Timothy for his own part must be faithful. He must seek, too, not merely to win good opinions from his fellow-men, but to satisfy **God** ; he must so act as to stand before God in the end **as a workman with no need to be ashamed.** This word may

glance back to **i.** 8, where Timothy was told not to be ashamed of his testimony. But it ought rather to be taken in a wider sense. There can be no worse shame than to be proved incompetent in your own proper work, and this applies to the Christian teacher as to every other workman.

In this comparison of the teacher to a **workman** the writer may have in mind some form of labour which is indicated in the latter part of the verse by the word **handle** (lit. 'cutting rightly'). The word occurs in the Septuagint translation of Prov. iii. 6 and x. 15, where it is applied to the hewing of a straight road or furrow. It might also be used of dividing something into just parts (e.g. a loaf of bread or a piece of cloth), and it has commonly been taken in this sense. The A.V. reads, 'rightly dividing the word of truth'—i.e. the teacher is exhorted, like a craftsman who can use his tools skilfully, to analyse each truth of scripture into its several elements, and so to apply it that there may be something for every hearer. From this interpretation of the verse the word ' orthotomy ' was adopted as a technical term for expounding a scripture text under its proper heads. But the passage is plainly meant to impress on Timothy that he must be a good servant of God, and not merely a keen logician ; and **the word of the Truth** is the Christian message as a whole—not some particular text or doctrine. If a definite craft is indicated, it is most probably that of a mason, which Paul suggests in his frequent references to ' edification '; as the mason hews the stones and fits them into each other, so the teacher must fashion his message into a structure that will stand foursquare. But perhaps we are to look for no specific metaphor. There are signs that in this word, as in others compounded in the same way, the idea of ' cutting ' had ceased to be essential, just as in our expression ' to put into good shape ' the notion of shaping is quite general. Moffatt's rendering may be accepted as adequate—**the way that you handle the word of the Truth.**

As a good workman, intent on the real issues of religion, 16 Timothy is to **avoid profane jargon.** The estimate of the new teaching as only empty talk is combined with the further one that it is **profane,** in the sense that it deals with holy things only to desecrate them. The word is applied in Heb. xii. 16 to Esau, who parted with a sacred privilege for the sake of a meal. Here it is similarly used for a materialistic type of thinking, to which spiritual facts are in no way different from those of common life. **For it leads people still further into irreligion.** Those teachers claimed to 'lead further,' to represent a more advanced type of Christian thinking. An interesting illustration may be found in 2 John 9 (**anyone who is ' advanced ' and will not remain by the doctrine of Christ**). Apparently the heretics called themselves ' the advanced party ' or ' the progressives ' ; and this name is taken up ironically, alike in 2 John and in the present Epistle. Those teachers indeed ' progress,' from one degree of **irreligion** to another ! Not only do they themselves progress in a wrong direction, but they 17 start a mischief which infects an ever larger circle ; **their doctrine spreads** (lit. ' eats in ') **like a gangrene.** The community in which they work is compared to a body, once healthy, in which a spreading sore has begun. Two of them are expressly named, **Hymenaeus and Philetus, who have failed in the Truth.** These appear to have been two heretical teachers connected with the Ephesian Church. They must have belonged to the time of Paul, since he is here represented as naming them ; but they had begun a movement which was probably still active when this Epistle was written. Philetus is only known from the mention of him here. **Hymenaeus** appears in 1 Tim. i. 20, where it is said that Paul had excommunicated him. Since there is no trace of this in the present verse, it has been inferred that the second Epistle to Timothy must be prior to the first—written at a time before the Church had taken serious measures to expel the heretics. This argument, however, is not conclusive. Hymenaeus, though excommunicated, may still have been carrying on his mischievous work.

An illustration is now given of the manner in which the two heretics have ' gone wrong concerning the truth,' and it is of special interest and importance as the one definite notice to be found in the Epistles as to the nature of the false teaching. 18 Those men say that ' **the resurrection has taken place already.**'

In what sense did they hold this belief ? There have been various millennarian movements in which it has been maintained that Christ had returned, in some secret place and manner, so that the last days have now actually begun. But if this were the heresy meant, we should have expected an emphasis on the Parousia or the Kingdom, not on the Resurrection. According to Irenaeus (I. 23. 5 ; cf. Justin, *Apol.*, 26), the heretic Menander taught that by receiving his baptism his followers would secure themselves against death, and a similar promise has been held out, from time to time, by fanatical leaders. In the present passage, however, the doctrine seems to be a broader one, to the effect that the general resurrection has already happened. The idea may have been that this life itself, in which the soul was reborn out of some previous life and death, was the true resurrection. Or more probably the Christian doctrine was interpreted in a purely spiritual sense ; since by faith in Christ men enter into immortal life, the resurrection will not come after death but has already taken place. This view is to some extent represented in the Fourth Gospel, with its repeated emphasis on a transition even in the present from death to life. One has only to think of the great passage, ' I am the Resurrection and the Life ' (John xi. 25), which rests on the belief that Christ's people receive their immortality here and now. On this side of his thought the evangelist was probably touched by gnostic influence, and in the gnostic sects the idea would no doubt be held in a cruder and more literal form.

The effect of this teaching was to **undermine** (or ' overturn ') **some people's faith.** In the Pastorals wrong faith is invariably conjoined with some wrong kind of practice, and it may be assumed that the new doctrine of the resurrection had resulted in loose living. This, indeed, is clearly indicated by the moral exhortation which follows. In the confidence that the resurrection was now past, some morbid ideas as to the bodily life would spring up, as in most of the gnostic sects. The body and its lusts would be treated as indifferent, in the belief that Christians had escaped from the flesh and could no longer be subdued by it. In contrast to those whose faith had been

thus undermined are those in whom it rests on a basis which
19 cannot be shaken. **The solid foundation laid by God remains.**
This ' foundation ' has sometimes been identified with Christ
Himself, or with the true Christian teaching, or with God's
eternal law, but, in view of the words which follow, it appears
to be the group of genuine Christians who form the rock on
which Christ will build His Church. It was customary for a
foundation-stone to bear an inscription, recording the name
of the builder or the character and purpose of the building.
So the community of God's people has ' this seal '—i.e. the
signature of God Himself, with a double motto : (a) ' The
Lord knows who are His.' These words are suggested by a
passage in Numbers (xvi. 5), in which Moses declares that God
will discriminate between those who are faithful to Him and
those who have rebelled with Korah. In view of this Old
Testament reminiscence about God caring **for His own,** it is
unnecessary to seek a reference to the doctrine of predestination. The meaning is simply that God knows the hearts of
men and can discern those who truly believe in Him (cf. Matt.
vii. 23). Another motto (b) is inscribed on the stone : **Let
everyone who names the name of the Lord give up evil.** Old
Testament language may here be combined with Jesus' own
saying (Luke xiii. 25–27), ' Depart from Me, ye who work
iniquity.' This second motto is meant to explain the first.
God knows (or cares for) His own people, and He knows them
to be His when their confession of His name has its outcome in
practical goodness. Taken as a whole, therefore, the passage
means that, while many have been perverted by false teaching,
there is still a solid body of believing men who form the
foundation of the Church. They hold to the true Christian
doctrine, and their practice agrees with their faith.

PERSONAL DIRECTIONS (ii. 20–26)

20 In any great house there are indeed vessels not only of gold
    and silver but also of wood and clay, some for noble, some
21   for menial service. If one will only keep clear of the
    latter, he will be put to noble use, he will be consecrated

and useful to the Owner of the House, he will be set apart
for good work of all kinds. So shun the lusts of youth and 22
aim at integrity, faith, love and peace, in the company of
those who invoke the Lord out of a pure heart.
Shut your mind against foolish, popular controversy ; be sure 23
that only breeds strife. And the Lord's servant must not 24
be a man of strife ; he must be kind to everybody, a skilled
teacher, a man who will not resent injuries ; he must be 25
gentle in his admonitions to the opposition—perhaps God
will let them change their mind and admit the Truth ;
they may come to their senses again and escape the snare of 26
the devil, as they are brought back to life by God to do His
will.

Timothy had been enjoined (in verse 15) to offer himself as
the type of a faithful teacher. He is now shown how he must
do so. The general counsels are made personal, and are
applied to the special situation in which Timothy finds
himself. **In any great house :** the simile of a foundation is 20
naturally followed up by that of the house which is built on it.
This is the more natural as the Church is repeatedly compared
in these Epistles to a house over which God presides (cf. 1 Tim.
iii. 15). **There are vessels not only of gold and silver but also of
wood and clay.** The language is borrowed from 1 Cor. iii. 12,
but while Paul there speaks of different kinds of work, some
more valuable than others, the reference here is to different
kinds of workers. Just as in a large house there must be vessels
for every purpose, so the Church must include all sorts and
conditions of men. The allusion to **vessels for noble and menial
service** is also taken from Paul (Rom. ix. 21) who likens God to
a potter, making vessels for different uses according to his
pleasure. In the present passage the simile is somewhat inept.
When Paul points out (1 Cor. xii. 23f.) that some members of
the body are less honourable than others, he is careful to show
that all are equally necessary and depend on one another.
The thought that in a great house all sorts of vessels are
required ought to lead up to a similar moral ; but in place of it
there is the reflection that the baser vessels are worthless. If

21 that is so, why are they there at all ? **If one will only keep clear of the latter.** Grammatically this should mean separation from the ' base vessels '—i.e. unworthy men ; and some would find here a warning against association with heretics, or doubtful members of the Church. But the phrase, ' purge,' or ' cleanse ' oneself, points to inward purification. A Christian must keep free of those evil thoughts and practices which cause certain men to be unworthy of their place in the ' great House '; **so he will be put to noble use, he will be consecrated and useful to the Owner of the House.** It has to be admitted that the clumsy simile becomes ever more confused as it goes on. The writer seems to forget that a vessel designed for a base use does not, by being washed, become fit for a higher one ; much less does a vessel made of earthenware change into gold. There is also an abrupt transition from household utensils to sacrificial vessels in a temple, and from that again to serviceable tools. The idea is plain enough—that in the Church there are good and bad members, and that Timothy must strive to be a Christian worthy of the name. But to express this idea the writer has borrowed from Paul language which was meant for another purpose. In so doing he finds himself compelled to identify degrees of honour with moral excellence and defect, and tries in vain to escape from the inconsistencies in which this involves him.

22 **So shun the lusts of youth.** Again (as in 1 Tim. iv. 12) Timothy is regarded as a young man, although at the close of Paul's life he must have been nearing forty. The ' lusts ' against which he is warned are not, however, merely the passions incident to hot-blooded youth. They are contrasted with **integrity, faithfulness, love and peace,** qualities which do not spring from sudden impulse but belong to a formed, consistent character. The thought is that Timothy ought now to be aiming at moral maturity. He has reached a stage when a settled habit of mind should take the place of flighty enthusiasms. This is brought out by the added words **in the company of those who invoke the Lord out of a pure heart.** Timothy must have in him the new moral temper which comes through Christian discipline and companionship ;

he must acquire the virtues which belong to Christ's people, as distinguished from all other men. The phrase ' call on the Lord ' is one that is often met with in the book of Acts and in Paul's Epistles, and suggests the invocation of Christ in prayer. It is hard to tell whether actual prayer was offered to Christ, or whether He was only called on to intercede with God—as we still pray ' in the name of Christ.' But the original meaning, whatever it may have been, fell into the background, and the phrase was used in a general sense to denote followers of Christ. For more than a century the term ' Christian,' invented by pagans and used, perhaps, in derision, was avoided by the Christians themselves, and various equivalents were put in its place. This, from a very early time, was one of them.

Along with the warning against hasty, impulsive action, there is a further caution against **foolish, popular controversy** 23 (lit. ' uneducated ' or ' ill-mannered debate '). The writer of the Pastorals is always concerned that the Christian teacher should conduct himself with proper dignity. Attempts will be constantly made to draw him into discussions, but he must not allow himself to become a mere platform debater. Controversy is **foolish** since it usually leads nowhere, and the argument which begins with due gravity is apt to finish in vulgar abuse on both sides. Not only is such controversy degrading, but it defeats its own purpose, since it **only breeds strife**, which is contrary to the very nature of the gospel. **The** 24 **Lord's servant must not be a man of strife.** Every Christian is ' the Lord's servant,' but Paul had applied the term to himself, in a special sense, as an apostle working in the service of Christ. So here it means the Christian teacher, whose task is to win men over, and who will accomplish nothing if he tries to coerce them. He must be **kind to everybody**, bent on **teaching** (as opposed to scolding and contradicting), ' **patient** ' **under injuries**, instead of getting angry and striking back, **gentle in his admonitions** (lit. ' educating with gentleness ') to 25 those who oppose him (a vague word is purposely used so as to include all adversaries, both within and without the Church). The emphasis falls on the idea of education. Men cannot be brought to the gospel by violent methods. They must be reasoned with and persuaded, and this must be done in a spirit of gentleness. By thus dealing with them, the teacher will not only gain their attention, but will make room for the operation of God's own power. Even the bitterest opponents, if they are treated patiently, will perhaps be led to change their mind and admit the Truth.

This lenient attitude towards enemies of the gospel is very striking, especially when we contrast it with the invectives of the Epistle of Jude and the book of Revelation. It may possibly indicate that our Epistle belongs to a time or a locality in which controversial passions had not been fully aroused. But in any case something must be allowed to the writer himself. He appears throughout as a man of calm, sagacious, and truly Christian spirit ; and this is nowhere more evident than in the present passage, where he deals with opponents who were often irritating and objectionable. There can be no doubt that his counsel was the right one, but it was many centuries before the Church learned his lesson ; perhaps we have not learned it yet.

The next section is notoriously difficult, owing to the slip-
26 shod manner in which the thought is expressed. **They may come to their senses again and escape the snares of the devil.** Thus far the meaning is clear, but the difficulty lies in the next words, which read literally ' having been captured by him unto his will.' To whom do the words ' him ' and ' his ' refer ? The most natural sense might seem to be that they escape the devil's snare after he has entrapped them and forced them to do his will. Another interpretation is that preferred by Moffatt : ' they escape after they have been captured by God to do His will.' This, however, would yield a very strange simile. They would be described as escaping one snare by falling into another. The word which Moffatt translates **brought back to life** cannot properly bear this meaning. It is a hunting term for catching a wild beast alive, and the writer would certainly have used some other word if he had wished to say that God rescues the devil's captives. Against both interpretations there is the objection that ' him ' and ' his ' are represented in Greek by two different pronouns : ' this one '

and ' that one.' By his employment of these two terms the writer seems purposely to distinguish two agents—the devil and God. It is best, on the whole, to translate the verse : ' God may grant them to escape from the snare of the devil after they have been captured by him, so as to do His will '— i.e. the will of God. Those who have erred in the faith are compared to birds or animals caught in a snare. Under wise persuasion and the action of God's Spirit they are enabled to escape, and to regain the liberty which consists in doing the will of God. By this interpretation the idea of ' coming to their senses ' is brought out in its full meaning. The accept-ance of false doctrine, as the writer sees it, is due to a tem-porary madness or delusion. The man who accepts the truth has returned to his right mind.

.   .   .   .

Thus far the instructions have been general in their nature. Timothy has been appointed to carry on the work of Paul, maintaining the true gospel, as Paul had done, in face of the evil and opposition which it must always encounter. He is now warned that a new and more difficult task lies before him. A time is close at hand when all the present evils will be heightened. Timothy must brace himself for a struggle in which he will need all his strength if he is to keep the Church faithful to Paul's message.

The conditions of this coming time are described by way of prediction, but the writer is plainly dealing with the situation of his own day. Speaking as he does in the character of Paul, he represents Paul as making a forecast of existing evils, much as the apocalyptic writers portray the times they live in as foreseen in visions by ancient prophets. The form of the passage is probably suggested by Paul's address to the elders of Ephesus in Acts xx. 18–35. This address itself, though based on something that Paul actually said, is no doubt coloured by Luke's knowledge of subsequent events.

A PERIOD OF MORAL DISSOLUTION PREDICTED (iii. 1–9)

iii.

1–2 Mark this, there are hard times coming in the last days. For men will be selfish, fond of money, boastful, haughty, abusive, disobedient to their parents, ungrateful, irreverent,

3 callous, relentless, scurrilous, dissolute, and savage ; they

4 will hate goodness, they will be treacherous, reckless and

5 conceited, preferring pleasure to God—for though they keep up a form of religion, they will have nothing to do

6 with it as a force. Avoid all such. Some of them worm their way into families and get hold of women-folk who feel crushed by the burden of their sins—wayward creatures

7 of impulse, always curious to learn and never able to

8 attain the knowledge of the Truth. For these guides of theirs are hostile to the Truth, just as Jannes and Jambres were hostile to Moses ; they are depraved in mind and

9 useless for any purpose of faith. However, they will get no further, for their abberation will be detected by every-one, as was the case with these magicians.

The great evil that is foreseen is the spread of dangerous heresy, but this growth of heresy is regarded as the outcome, in the religious sphere, of a general corruption. Hence in this introductory section a society is depicted in which all moral sanctions have broken down. There can be no right thinking when everything in man's life has become perverted.

1 The phrase **in the last days** is commonly used in the New Testament of the time immediately preceding the return of Christ and the end of the present world. This is doubtless in the writer's mind when he makes his prediction. He believes that the end of all things cannot be long delayed, and that the ruin which he foresees will be the final one. But this side of his thought is not made emphatic. When he speaks of **the last days** he refers to the future, when the evil tendencies already manifest will have reached their head. **There are hard times coming**—i.e. times which will be difficult for the Christian teacher because of the wickedness that will prevail.

2 For in this coming time **men will be selfish, fond of money.**

Here begins a long list of manifold forms of evil which will everywhere prevail ; but two vices are placed at the beginning, since the writer sees in them the roots of all the other perversions. Men will lose sight of all higher interests ; they will be wrapped up in themselves, and they will have no other aim in life than to amass money. In other words, the age approaching will be wholly materialistic, and the vices that ensue will be the poisonous weeds that grow naturally in such a soil. It is needless to look for any studied arrangement in the list that follows. The writer has apparently put down the names of vices as they happened to occur to him, mixing up the graver sins with others that are less serious. In several cases he seems to be guided in his arrangement by nothing else than an assonance in the Greek words. Similar lists are to be found in several of Paul's Epistles, and the passage in Rom. i. 30f. is evidently the model which is followed here. Such lists of vices, however, were a common feature in the ethical literature of the time, and were more particularly in favour with the Stoic moralists. In so far as any division can be made in the present passage it may be said that moral offences are viewed under four aspects : (1) sins against God (**ungrateful, irreverent**) ; (2) want of natural affection ; (3) wrongs to society (slanderers, **treacherous**) ; (4) vices of disposition (proud, **dissolute, savage**). By its very incoherence the catalogue leaves a powerful impression of moral anarchy. All standards have been lost. Men are tossed about helplessly by their baser passions. Religion still exists, but men hold to it only as a matter of custom, keeping up a form of religion, and disowning it **as a force.** Paul had spoken, in Rom. ii. 20, of the self-complacent Jew who claimed to possess the Law as ' the form of knowledge and truth '—i.e. the religion which gave perfect expression to God's will. This Pauline phrase is in the writer's mind, but he uses it to denote the externals of religion as opposed to the vital power. Through the whole passage we can trace a dependence on that first chapter of Romans, though Paul's account of the heathen world of his time is partly modified to suit later conditions. Some of the darker features of Paul's indictment are left out, but for this reason the picture is more accurate than that of Paul, which is certainly exaggerated. We know from many historical testimonies that the Roman world of the first century had by no means sunk into utter corruption. As always happens, the worst vices were confined to certain classes, at the top and the bottom of the social scale ; between them were vast numbers of clean-living and seriously minded men and women. Yet in that age there was undoubtedly a general lowering of the rules of conduct which even heathen morality had required, and it is this, more than a gross viciousness, which is described in the present chapter. The account, in pretty much all its details, would be recognized by any contemporary reader as true to fact.

Avoid (lit. ' turn away from ') **all such**—i.e. the people who conduct themselves in this way. The meaning is not so much that Timothy in his personal life should keep aloof from evil society, as that he should be careful about those whom he receives into the Church. It is his duty as a responsible leader to keep the Christian community pure. Those who are plainly infected with the prevailing vices must on no account be admitted to membership, for they will turn the privilege to mischievous purposes. A transition is thus made from the general corruption of the time to the particular evil of false doctrine which had invaded the Church. It always happens that when the moral atmosphere has become unwholesome there appear morbid types of religion. They may be sincerely held, but they arise from instincts and modes of thought which have grown perverted. This, as the writer perceives, was the true origin of the gnostic heresies, with their emphasis on the 6 sensual and occult. ' For of this sort '—i.e. produced by these heathen influences—are the men **who worm their way into families** : the suggestion is that these half-pagan teachers secure a footing in households of good position by underhand means. Such a household, in ancient times, included a great number of people, slaves and freedmen and distant connexions, as well as the parents and children. The most effective method of propaganda was to win over someone in a wealthy household, all of whose members were constantly thrown together. The false teachers sought particularly to make converts among the women, who had time on their hands and were easily attracted by something new. Their first object was to **get hold of** (lit. ' to lead into captivity ') **the women-folk.** In Greek this is a diminutive expressing contempt, and is aptly rendered in the old translation ' silly women '; only, the idea conveyed is not so much the want of brains, as the want of all moral substance. These women **are** burdened with sins, **wayward creatures of impulse.** Living idly for their own pleasures, they have gone from bad to worse, so that their characters have fallen to pieces, and they now lie at the mercy of every chance desire. They are **always curious to** 7 **learn, and never able to attain the knowledge of the Truth.** The women in question are not ' silly ' in the sense that they have no minds worth speaking of. On the contrary they are highly intelligent, and always on the quest for novel ideas. But their whole motive is to get new thrills. Since they have no serious purpose they are incapable of grasping any truth, least of all the gospel, which for this writer is emphatically **the Truth.** The passage is one of acute insight and observation, and is still faithful to life. Eccentric doctrines of any kind—religious, social, medical, educational—make their chief appeal to well-to-do, idle women, on the look-out for new sensations. It remains true, likewise, that a dissipated life often goes along with a certain religiosity. Sentimental playwrights and novelists have extracted a great deal of cheap pathos from this fact, but the author of the Pastorals takes another and healthier view. He has just as little sympathy for the dissolute women who cultivate religion along with their other excitements as he has for the dishonest teachers who prey upon them, and whom he compares with **Jannes and** 8 **Jambres who were hostile to Moses.** According to a Jewish legend, preserved in the Targums, these were Egyptian magicians who sought to rival the miracles performed by Moses (Exod. vii. 11 ; ix. 11). There was apparently an ancient book devoted to their exploits, and allusions to them are found even in classical literature, so that the writer can assume that his readers will understand the allusion. The point of comparison is a double one. Like the Egyptian sorcerers, the false teachers are bound to fail, and like them they act from evil motives. **They are depraved in mind and useless for any purpose of faith.** They cannot produce faith in others since they do not have it themselves. ' The faith ' in these Epistles is usually another name for the Christian religion ; but since it is here coupled with intelligence it must denote a personal quality—the faith which is necessary for apprehending the gospel. These men, like the ' silly women ' whom they mislead, are incapable of true knowledge, both mentally and 9 spiritually. **However, they will get no further, or, ' will not progress any more.'** As in verse 16 of the preceding chapter, there seems to be a reference to the claim of these teachers to stand for a ' progressive ' Christianity ; and the writer plays on the word. He says satirically that in the matter of making converts they will not be ' progressive ' much longer. **For their aberration** (lit. their ' madness ' or ' folly ') **will be detected by everyone, as was the case with these** magicians. No doubt there is here a reference to the legendary tale, from which the names of Jannes and Jambres are borrowed. After describing how they tried, by their juggling, to discredit Moses, it would tell how they were finally overtaken by a shameful exposure. This, it is said here, will happen very soon to those pretentious teachers. The prediction may be made on the general ground that all imposture is certain in the end to be unmasked. Or the writer may have in his mind some definite incident, well known to his readers, of the detection of a professed wonder-worker. He would say in effect, as has often been said when a glaring fraud among spiritualists or theosophists has been exposed, ' it will be impossible now for any sensible person to believe in these practices.'

In view of what has happened, or will shortly happen, to those deceivers, Timothy is warned to keep before him the example of Paul, whom he has personally known. The false teachers had met with momentary success, followed by disgrace. Paul, on the other hand, had been misunderstood and persecuted, but had always come through triumphantly.

This is sure to be the experience of all who teach the gospel in his spirit.

PAUL AS THE EXAMPLE OF A TRUE TEACHER (iii. 10-13)

Now you have followed my teaching, my practice, my aims, 10
my faith, my patience, my love, my stedfastness, my 11
persecutions, my sufferings—all that befell me at Antioch,
Iconium and Lystra, all the persecutions that I had to
undergo, from which the Lord rescued me. (Yes, and all 12
who would live the religious life in Christ Jesus will be
persecuted.) Bad characters and impostors will go from 13
bad to worse, deceiving others and deceived themselves.

Now you (as contrasted with those others) **have followed** 10
my teaching. The word used of Timothy's discipleship is a
pregnant one, implying that he had not only been Paul's
companion, but had carefully noted all that he had seen and
heard. Along with Paul's teaching Timothy had followed or
studied his personal behaviour, his **practice, aims, faith, patience,
love, stedfastness.** The qualities selected are those which
still impress us as we examine the career of Paul—his indomit-
able will, directed to a single aim, the purity of his motives, his
unfailing consideration for others even when they had sorely
tried him. Timothy had seen Paul's character tested by 11
persecutions and sufferings; and the nature of these is
indicated by episodes of his life which Timothy himself had
witnessed—**all that befell me at Antioch** (i.e. Antioch in
Pisidia), **Iconium, and Lystra, all the persecutions I had to
undergo.** It is strange that mention is made only of that
period in Paul's life when Timothy, as a young man in his
native city of Lystra, had first come in contact with him.
Since then he had been in constant association with Paul for
years together, and had seen his heroism under far greater
trials than those of that distant time. The intention may be
to remind Timothy of how he had first been attracted to Paul
by his patience under hardships. The truth of the message
had been attested by the conduct of the messenger, and the

LE 123

support which Christ had given him. All that he had afterwards seen of Paul had only confirmed that first impression.
12 Paul's experience will repeat itself in **all who would** (lit. ' want
to ') **live the religious life** (lit. ' to live piously ') **in Christ
Jesus.** A strong emphasis is laid on ' piously,' which here
implies, as it always does in the Pastorals, a genuine faith
combined with strenuous Christian living. One might almost
translate, ' all who resolve to be Christians in real earnest.'
The phrase ' in Christ,' which Paul uses constantly and almost
always with the suggestion of a mystical union with Christ, is
rare in the Pastorals (cf. 1 Tim. i. 14 ; 2 Tim. ii. 1, 10), where
it appears to be borrowed from Paul, with little sense of its
deeper import. It here serves merely to distinguish the
Christian mode of life from the Jewish or pagan. The writer
lives in a time when the persecution of Christianity had fairly
begun. He says that Christians who are serious in their religion
are sure to be persecuted, and that those who are left alone
by the hostile world are marked out, by that very fact, as
lukewarm or counterfeit. It might seem as if they fared
better than their suffering brethren, but this is only in appear-
13 ance ; for **bad characters and impostors will go on from bad
to worse.** Here again there seems to be an ironical reference
to the ' progress ' on which the false teachers prided themselves. It has just been said that the true Christian will be
persecuted, and in contrast with this we should expect ' the
unfaithful Christian will enjoy comfort and success.' This is
what the writer means, but, by a sudden turn of thought, he
makes it ' they will advance themselves—towards the worse.'
Their prosperity will be only apparent, and the more it
increases the more they are storing up trouble. The reference
is to all bad Christians, but it is still the false teachers who are
uppermost in the writer's mind. He calls them **impostors**
(lit. ' sorcerers '), in view of the comparison with the Egyptian
magicians. No doubt the comparison was partly suggested
by the fact that magic was a prominent feature in some forms
of gnosticism. By artifices which seemed to prove supernatural power, the teachers gained much of their influence.
This exercise of magic is probably implied in the closing words

deceiving others and deceived themselves. It very often happens that those who practise fraud on others are at last deluded by their own pretence ; falsehood has become so much their element that they lose the power of distinguishing it from truth. So the writer, who has begun by denouncing the impostors, ends on a note of pity. If they victimize other people, they are themselves in the end the chief victims.

THE CHRISTIAN TESTIMONY SUPPORTED BY SCRIPTURE (iii. 14–16)

But hold you to what you have been taught, hold to your convictions, remember who your teachers were, remember how 15 you have known from childhood the sacred writings that can impart saving wisdom by faith in Christ Jesus. All 16 scripture is inspired by God and profitable for teaching, for reproof, for amendment, and for moral discipline, to make 17 the man of God proficient and equip him for good work of every kind.

Timothy is to look to Paul's teaching and example ; but he is not wholly dependent on the witness of Paul. He has been nurtured on the Scriptures, which contain the will of God Himself, and which confirm what has been learned from the other teachers. **Hold to what you have been taught, hold to 14 your convictions.** As against those who ' progress,' towards the better, as they claim, but really towards the worse, Timothy is to hold fast to what he has. Since he is satisfied that Paul's message is true, he must not move away from it ; and there are two things which will confirm him in his stand. In the first place he can **remember who** his **teachers were.** He has learned his religion not from chance adventurers, but from those whose characters he knew and trusted. The reference is chiefly to Paul himself, whose qualities and sufferings have just been described ; but with Paul are included the mother and grandmother mentioned in i. 5, and other devoted Christians. Yet there is a further ground of confidence in that **you have 15 known from childhood the sacred writings** (lit. ' sacred letters '). According to the custom of pious Jewish homes, Timothy had been trained from his earliest days in Bible knowledge ; and this is doubtless the meaning of the verse. But the term used for **writings** is not the ordinary one for the Scriptures. It denotes properly ' letters,' either in the sense of alphabetic characters, or in the wider sense, which it also bears in English, of ' literature.' Several reasons may be conjectured as to why this peculiar word is employed : (1) It may take up, in a half-playful manner, the thought of how Timothy was educated when still an infant. He learned to read, he was taught his very letters, from the Scriptures. (2) It may enforce the contrast between Timothy and the false teachers, and in this case a strong emphasis would rest on the word **sacred**. The other teachers had busied themselves with various books, many of them of a very doubtful nature. Timothy had given his whole time to the study of the one sacred book. (3) Most probably the term is chosen in order to denote sacred literature in its full extent. Timothy was familiar not only with the Bible itself, but with books relating to it—the apocryphal and apocalyptic books which were cherished both by Jews and Christians, perhaps the Christian writings which were now coming into existence, although none of them were yet regarded as Scripture. This would give point to the subsequent reference to ' inspired scripture ' as opposed to ' sacred literature ' in general. A more exact meaning would also be given to the words immediately following, **that can impart saving wisdom** (lit. ' sharpen the mind unto salvation '). This would be a strange way of describing the Bible, which was conceived as the very word of God ; but it would well apply to books written about religion by wise and holy men. Although such books may carry no authority, they give the right attitude of mind, the mood and understanding by which the Bible itself can be understood. At the same time they cannot lead to saving knowledge unless they are read through **faith in Christ Jesus**—i.e. the faith in Christ must be present to illuminate and vitalize the written word.

16   The next passage has played a memorable part in theological debate as the chief proof-text of the inspiration of Scripture. It does not, as has often been affirmed, involve a doctrine of

verbal inspiration. The crucial word means literally ' breathed into by God '—i.e. a Divine quality is present in Scripture, distinguishing it from all human utterance. Ordinary language as used in the Bible becomes the vehicle of a message from God. A wrong meaning, too, has often been read into the words **all scripture.** This has been taken as ' the whole of scripture,' implying that everything stated in the Bible, however contrary to reason or known fact, must be accepted as Divine truth. But this explanation of the words is forbidden by the rules of Greek grammar. **All scripture** is ' every scripture '—each one of those writings which together make up our Bible. Nothing is said of their contents in detail. The idea is simply that each of the sacred books has something to reveal to us of the mind of God. Since this is the meaning, we ought, most probably, to take the reference to inspiration in an attributive sense, translating, not as Moffatt has done, **all scripture is inspired,** but rather ' every inspired scripture.' A contrast is drawn between ordinary religious books, even the ' sacred literature ' mentioned in the previous verse, and those books which had been set apart as authoritative. To a Greek ear the word ' scripture ' conveyed no idea but that of a ' writing ' ; and the adjective ' inspired ' is attached to it to guard against possible misunderstanding. The writer then proceeds to describe the value of those holy books in which Timothy has been trained since childhood. It must be noted that nothing is said of a mysterious virtue inhering in the mere words of Scripture. The object is to show how a devout and intelligent teacher may so expound every biblical writing as to improve his hearers. **Every inspired Scripture is profitable for teaching, for reproof.** This applies to the teacher's work on its doctrinal side. Basing himself on Scripture, he can impart the right message and confute all false opinions. Likewise the Bible will serve him **for amendment and for moral discipline.** Here it is meant that in practical exhortation, as in the exposition of doctrine, he can always draw on the storehouse of biblical wisdom. At the time when this passage was written, the Old Testament was still the one Bible of the Church, and here perhaps we must find the reason for the stress laid on ' every part of scripture.' The question would often arise (as it has constantly done since), whether large portions of the ancient book might not be discarded as useless for Christian purposes. Probably the gnostics had already begun their effort to have the Old Testament abandoned altogether. This writer takes the position, not only that the Old Testament is the word of God, but that every part of it, when rightly handled by a wise teacher, can be used in the service of the gospel. Although the Law and the Prophets were before Christ, they yet pointed 17 to His coming and foreshadowed His message. A full knowledge of them is the necessary preparation for the work of Christian instruction, **to make the man of God proficient** (lit. 'fit for his task'). The phrase 'man of God' also occurs in I Tim. vi. II, where it may be understood in the general sense of 'Christian' as well as in the more definite one. Here it seems to be used emphatically of a religious teacher, who must be trained in the Scriptures before he is properly qualified for his work. The phrase itself is an Old Testament one, applied to a prophet as a man who speaks in the name of God. It here carries the suggestion that the Christian teacher stands in the line of the prophets. He is entrusted with a message from God, and must be able to enforce it from the Divine book. The concluding words, '**equipped for good work of every kind**,' occur several times in the Epistles (2 Tim. ii. 21 ; I Tim. v. 10 ; Titus iii. I). They here serve to define the previous reference to the 'fitness' of the man of God, and to make it still clearer that his work must be of a manifold nature. The teacher who expounds and defends Christian doctrine must also be able to apply it practically to the various needs of life. For the whole task which is laid on him he will find his most powerful aid in a thorough knowledge of Scripture.

TIMOTHY IS IMPLORED TO BE STEDFAST (iv. 1–5)

iv.

1 In presence of God and of Christ Jesus who will judge the living and the dead, in the light of His appearance and His reign, 2 I adjure you to preach the word ; keep at it in season and out of season, refuting, checking and exhorting men ;

never lose patience with them, and never give up your
teaching ; for the time will come when people decline to be 3
taught sound doctrine, they will accumulate teachers to
suit themselves and tickle their own fancies, they will give 4
up listening to the Truth and turn to myths.

Whatever happens, be self-possessed, flinch from no suffering, 5
do your work as an evangelist, and discharge all your
duties as a minister.

The duties of a Christian leader have been defined in the
preceding chapter, and a solemn appeal is now made to
Timothy to discharge them faithfully. **In presence of God** 1
and of Christ Jesus. The same impressive formula is found in
1 Tim. v. 21, but is here used with peculiar fitness, since Paul is
supposed to be giving his last sacred charge, on the eve of death.
Christ is called to witness as the future **Judge of the living and**
the dead, as one, therefore, who will not only know whether
promises are kept, but will call to account him who breaks
them. Timothy is further adjured by **the appearance and**
reign of Christ. Elsewhere the ' Epiphany ' is the appearance
of Christ on earth (cf. 1 Tim. vi. 14). Here, as in Titus ii. 13, it
is His return in glory, and is coupled with the Kingdom on
which He will then enter and which His people will share with
Him. The dearest hope of the Christian is to have part in that
Kingdom, and Timothy is warned to do his duty, on pain of
losing this supreme goal of the Christian life. The appearing
and the Kingdom are not to be taken as synonymous. In one
case the thought is of the Judgment, in the other of the eternal
life bestowed on the righteous. Each man will be judged by his
works, and the work to which Timothy is so solemnly exhorted 2
is to **preach the word ; keep at it** (lit. ' stand at attention ') **in**
season and out of season. This may mean ' whether you are in
the mood or not,' and such an interpretation would carry out
the image of a soldier holding himself prepared at all hours and
under all conditions to do his duty. But in view of the verse
that follows it seems necessary to apply the words not to
Timothy himself, but to his hearers; ' whether the opportunity
is favourable or not '—i.e. even in the face of bitter opposition.

Refuting, checking and exhorting, means the preacher's task as viewed in three different aspects, involving an appeal to the reason, the conscience, and the will. Timothy is to proclaim a message in which all these elements are included, and he is never to lose patience and never to give up teaching. The thought seems here to be the same as in ii. 25. Although his hearers may be opposed to him, Timothy is not to lose his temper. He must not dictate but teach, and must do so with 3 unwearied patience. For the time will come when they will not bear with sound doctrine. The previous reference to ' in time and out of time ' is here explained. It is implied that at present the opportunity is not unfavourable. Men are inclined to listen to the gospel, and Timothy finds his work comparatively easy and pleasant. But in coming days the teacher who upholds the genuine Christian message (the ' healthy teaching ') will meet with hard opposition. The writer is thinking of his own day, but looks at it, with the eyes of Paul, as still in the future. In these coming days men will accumulate teachers to suit themselves. They will no longer be content to follow one teacher, who stands for the one true gospel ; tired of the old discipline, they will give scope to all their caprices, and will break into various sects, each with its own particular oracle. To suit themselves is thrown in with a touch of contempt. They will have heaps of teachers, all of their own choosing, and with no other credentials. The contempt is still more evident in the added words, to tickle their own fancies (lit. ' having an itch in their hearing '). All they ask of a teacher will be the passing sensation of listening to something new. Whether the message is true or not will matter little, so long as it excites them pleasantly for the moment. The result will be that they will give up listening to the Truth—i.e. to the genuine gospel. For the very reason that it is true, it will seem dull and commonplace and cease to interest them; in place of it they will turn to myths. Reference has been made already to those ' old wives' fables,' apparently Jewish legends, in which the heretical teachers delighted. The term is used here, however, to describe not so much the origin of the new teaching as its emptiness and folly. When men give up their old faith, they do not fall into mere indifference. They still need something to hold by, and they replace what they have lost with some other belief, usually with one that is palpably childish and false.

Whatever happens, be self-possessed (lit. ' But for your part be sober ') ; do not try like those others to be sensational for the sake of novelty. **Flinch from no suffering, such as will come to you from your faithfulness. Do your work as an evangelist.** In the time of Paul the word ' evangelist ' denoted a special office, different from that of a prophet or teacher (cf. Acts xxi. 8 ; Eph. iv. 11). It seems latterly to have lost this technical significance, and is here used in its literal sense of one who announces the gospel. Timothy is to make this his calling, and confine himself to it. If he does everything that is required of a faithful teacher, he will have no time or desire for doubtful speculations. This is indicated in the next words, in which Timothy is reminded that his ministry entails a wide range of **duties.** If he preaches the gospel in the right spirit, he will find employment for every gift and energy he may possess.

The Farewell (iv. 6–8)

The last drops of my own sacrifice are falling ; my time to go 6 has come. I have fought in the good fight ; I have run 7 my course ; I have kept the faith. Now the crown of a good 8 life awaits me, with which the Lord, that just Judge, will reward me on the great Day—and not only me but all who have loved and longed for His appearance.

In this passage the Epistle reaches its climax. Paul has now bestowed his last counsels on Timothy and appointed him as his successor ; nothing remains but to bid him good-bye. The passage is a noble and touching one. For its own sake it holds a cherished place in the memory of the Church ; besides, it illuminates the whole Epistle and brings out the purpose for which it was written. Paul has been set before us as the pattern of the true missionary. Those who come after him are to take their inspiration from his message, his career, and his martyr's death. In all things they are to make it their one aim to follow in the footsteps of the great apostle.

6 'For I am already being consecrated.' The whole passage depends on the 'I' which stands emphatically at the beginning. Paul himself can now do no more ; his great work, if it is to go forward, must be taken up by his successors. The metaphor employed is a bold and impressive one, but is capable of several explanations. A word is used which means literally 'I am being poured out,' and obviously has reference to the ancient custom of pouring a libation over the victim which is about to be sacrificed. Paul himself makes use of the metaphor in Phil. ii. 17 ; 'but even if I am poured out over the sacrifice and offering of your faith.' He there thinks of his blood, shed in martyrdom, as a libation which will consecrate the service rendered to God by his converts. The meaning here may be the same. Paul thinks of his approaching death as the solemn libation by which all later missionaries will feel themselves to be dedicated. Moffatt takes the words in this sense, and aptly translates the last drops of my own sacrifice are falling. The idea thus expressed may find support from the parallel passage in Philippians. But Paul could hardly speak in this fashion of a sacrifice which was still in the future. Moreover, he is not speaking of a sacrifice, but of the preliminary libation, and of one which has reference to himself, not to the Church after him. He is the victim which is being prepared. In other words, he thinks of the experiences through which he is now passing—his last days in prison, his trial, and the inevitable sentence—as the prelude to a coming sacrifice. 'Already the libation is being poured over me' as over a sacrificial victim—i.e. 'my death is just imminent.' The same thought is expressed in the further metaphor : 'the time of my departure has come.' A word is used which means literally a 'loosening' or 'breaking up' (the English word 'analysis' is this Greek one borrowed). The idea involved may be that of a traveller breaking up his tent before the new day's march ; or that of a sailor casting loose the rope as he puts out to sea. It has been suggested that, if this latter

meaning is intended, the previous words may refer to the practice of pouring a libation to the sea-gods before commencing a voyage. In that case, however, the metaphor would be hopelessly confused ; Paul would speak of himself as at once the libation and the departing ship. Most likely, when these Epistles were written, the word had lost its metaphorical sense and meant nothing more than the act of leaving on a long journey. Paul has now lived his life and is about to go. I **have fought in the good fight,** or, more properly, the wrestling 7 match. As so often in Paul's Epistles, the Christian is compared to an athlete contending for a prize. The force of his words may be brought out by our own phrase : ' I have played the game.' But the struggle is defined as the **good** or ' noble ' one, to distinguish it from all ordinary contests. It is the grandest one in which man can engage, and the prize at stake is of inestimable value. **I have run my course.** This also is a favourite Pauline metaphor, taken from the ancient games. To the previous idea of a hard task accomplished, the thought is added that the task was prescribed. A course had been marked out for the apostle, and now he has traversed it right on to the goal. This thought is made explicit in the next words, **I have kept the faith.** The Christian faith has already been compared to a deposit with which the servant of Christ is entrusted. Paul can feel that he has been loyal to his trust, and can now hand it on, unimpaired, to those who succeed him.

Now (lit. ' for the rest ') everything else is finished and only 8 one thing remains : **the crown of a good life awaits me.** With the image of the racecourse still in his mind, the writer uses a technical term. The prize to be contended for was ' laid up '— usually in a prominent place where it could be seen by competitors and onlookers. It consisted of a wreath, which in the present simile becomes a ' crown of righteousness.' This can hardly mean a crown composed of righteousness (as in the similar phrase a ' crown of life '). The point of the whole passage is that Paul, in his lifetime, has acquitted himself righteously, and, after his martyr's death, will receive his reward. Moffatt is no doubt right in translating **the crown of a good life ;** what it will consist in, the apostle does not know, but he is convinced that those who have done righteously will enter on some great joy which the Lord will award on the great Day, in the same manner as the president of the games bestows a wreath on the victor. To add force to this metaphor, the Lord is called ' that just Judge.' Christ is compared to an umpire whose decisions can be fully trusted ; and at the same time the idea is conveyed that Christ, who gives the prize for righteousness, has Himself lived the supremely righteous life, and will recompense those who have followed Him. This idea accounts for the next words : **and not only me but all who have loved and longed for His appearance.** Christ in the Judgment will acknowledge all His people. Perhaps the first intention was to write simply ' those who have loved Him,' but this thought is made more precise. The mark of Christians was that they looked for the return of Christ in glory, and one of the names by which they called themselves in the early days was ' those who waited for Christ ' (cf. Phil. iii. 20). It was this hope that the Lord was at hand which enabled them to bear up through all trial and opposition. To ' love His coming ' implies an eager longing for it, and Moffatt has emphasized this in his translation ; but the more comprehensive word is chosen in order to suggest that love for Christ Himself is the motive of the longing. The coming is yet in the future, but Christians live in the thought of it as if it were present, since they love Him who is to come again. Love is involved in the waiting, just as it is in the wistfulness with which you look for the return of a dear absent friend. It is therefore unnecessary to make the ' appearance ' refer here to the earthly life of Christ, on which Christians look back with love.

INSTRUCTIONS IN VIEW OF TIMOTHY'S VISIT (iv. 9–13)

9–10 Do your best to come soon to me, for Demas, in his love for this world has deserted me and gone to Thessalonica ; Crescens

11 is off to Gaul, Titus to Dalmatia, Luke is the only one who is with me. Pick up Mark and bring him along with you, for

12 he is useful in helping me. (I have had to send Tychicus to

Ephesus.) When you come, bring the mantle I left at 13
Troas with Carpus, also my books and particularly my
papers.

The main part of the letter has now come to an end, and the
closing sections consist of notices and greetings of a strictly
personal nature. They are of special interest, since it is here, if
anywhere in the Pastorals, that we find traces of Paul's own
hand. The letters as we have them have grown, most probably, out of fragments of Paul's correspondence, brief personal
notes which were not worth preserving as they were, and have
been used as the ground-work for the present writings. They
may well have been addressed to Timothy and Titus, but we
can only guess at the date and occasion on which they were
composed. That they are genuine Pauline fragments is more
than likely, in view not only of their language, which is
different from that of the Epistles as a whole, but also of the
difficulty of fitting them into their present context. This
becomes apparent when they are examined in detail.

Do your best to come soon to me. This request is indeed 9
surprising after the previous part of the letter. Nothing has
been said as to an expected visit from Timothy ; the assumption has been throughout that the two friends have parted for
ever, and, in the touching verses which have immediately
preceded, Paul has said that he is at the very point of laying
down his life. Yet here he writes to Timothy at Ephesus, asking
him to pay a promised visit. However speedily the appeal
might be answered, some months would have to elapse, under
ancient conditions of travel, before Paul's letter could reach
Ephesus and Timothy make his way to Rome. The request
for a visit is obviously out of place in the present letter. **For 10
Demas, in his love for this world, has deserted me.** In Col. iv.
14 greetings are sent from Demas, along with Luke and Aris-
tarchus. Nothing is known of him except from certain allusions in the apocryphal Acts of Paul and Thecla, which are
evidently coloured by the present passage. If the passage as a
whole is mainly from Paul's hand, the disparaging reference to
Demas has probably been inserted by the later writer, since it

connects with the previous words about those who have loved Christ's appearance. In contrast to those true disciples who wait for the heavenly Kingdom, Demas had preferred the present world. It may be conjectured that while Demas in Paul's lifetime had been zealous in the Christian cause, he had afterwards become lukewarm and had turned to worldly pursuits. When this Epistle was written, he was still remembered as the type of a renegade missionary. The original note of Paul may have read simply, ' Demas has gone to Thessalonica,' presumably on the work of the mission ; but, in view of the bad reputation he had acquired later, his going was construed as a desertion. **Crescens is off to Gaul, Titus to Dalmatia.** Of Crescens nothing is known ; and the reading ' Galatia ' is better attested than ' Gaul.' It is indeed hardly possible that Paul, or even a later author writing in his name, could have spoken off-handedly of Gaul as a natural field of labour for a Christian teacher. **Dalmatia** was part of Illyricum (on the east side of the Adriatic), and Paul declares, in Rom. xv. 19, that his work has extended to that region. Nothing is told us of this Illyrian mission, but Titus' visit to Dalmatia

11 may have been connected with it. **Luke is the only one who is with me.** It is to be noted that Paul is not here complaining that all his friends except Luke have abandoned him. He merely states the fact that he is at present short-handed, and would therefore like to have Timothy's assistance as soon as possible. His other workers have gone, apparently on his own orders, to various distant places. Naturally he has kept Luke beside him, since he is an ailing man and Luke is his physician. **Pick up Mark and bring him along with you.** The suggestion is that Mark was stationed at some place on the route which Timothy would follow. Paul wishes to have him, ' **for he is useful in helping me.**' It is doubtful whether this refers to personal service or to work in the mission. Probably the vagueness is intentional. Paul says in effect, ' I want Mark because he can turn his hand to anything.' From Col. iv. 10 ; Philem. 24, as well as from this passage, it is evident that Paul had now forgotten those objections to Mark which had led to his quarrel with Barnabas (Acts xv. 37f.). Barnabas

136

was clearly a good judge of men. He had been the first to see promise in Paul himself when others were dubious ; he had likewise believed in Mark when Paul was set against him. Everything we know of Barnabas confirms the description of him in the book of Acts as a ' generous man ' (Acts xi. 24).

' I have sent Tychicus to Ephesus.' **Tychicus** is known to us 12 as the messenger who carried the letters to Colossians and Ephesians, also as one of the Asian delegates who accompanied Paul on his final visit to Jerusalem (Acts xx. 4). It may be implied here that Tychicus is being sent to Ephesus to take Timothy's place during his absence ; or, as Moffatt suggests (**I have had to send**), Paul needs to have Mark since he had to part with Tychicus. **When you come, bring the mantle I left at** 13 **Troas with Carpus.** The cloak in question was that which the Romans called a *paenula*, and its Greek name is an adaptation of the Latin. It was little more than a blanket, with a hole in the middle for the head, and, since it was so easy to put on, was much used by soldiers and travellers. In hot weather, however, it was troublesome to carry, and Paul had apparently left it behind, with other pieces of his baggage, when he arrived at the port of Troas and set off on one of his journeys. There is some evidence that the name was also applied to a case or satchel for holding papers, and some have inferred, from the reference which follows, that this is the meaning here ; but the ordinary sense is the more likely. Along with the cloak, Timothy is to **bring my books, and particularly my papers** (lit. ' the parchments '). The books would be in the form of papyrus rolls, and it would be highly interesting to know what this travelling library of Paul consisted in. Would it include, for instance, one of those collections of the sayings of Jesus which preceded our present Gospels ? All conjecture is useless. The ' pieces of parchment ' are distinguished from the ordinary papyrus rolls. In those days, as now, parchment was used for official documents, which needed to resist a great deal of wear and tear. Moffatt is probably right in translating **my papers**— i.e. certificates which Paul carried about with him, for the purpose of proving, for instance, that he was a Roman citizen. The verse is trivial in itself, but has a very important bearing on the criticism of these Epistles. Between Paul's trial at Rome and his last passage through Troas there lay an interval of about six years, and by that time the missing cloak would hardly be worth recovering. These verses, therefore, may be assigned with some confidence to a letter written considerably earlier. We know that Paul passed through Troas on his last journey to Jerusalem, and it has been conjectured that he wrote this request from Caesarea just after his arrival, or during his imprisonment there shortly afterwards. Troas, however, is well to the north of Ephesus, and if he was summoned to Caesarea Timothy would travel south. If verses 9–13 belong to a separate note (and they can hardly be understood otherwise), it must have been written at some time during Paul's missionary career which we cannot now determine. We know definitely of three occasions when he was in Troas (Acts xvi. 8 ; xx. 5 ; 2 Cor. ii. 12), none of which can be fitted into the present context. But during the three years that he worked at Ephesus he may have had various occasions to be in the city, which was barely a hundred miles away, and which contained a flourishing Church of his foundation.

CAUTION AGAINST ALEXANDER (iv. 14–15)

14 Alexander the blacksmith has done me great harm : *the Lord*
15 *will pay him back for what he has done* (beware of him), for he has been bitterly hostile to anything I have said.

It is difficult to connect these two verses either with what precedes or with what follows. Possibly they were a postscript to the brief note of instructions (9–13). Or perhaps they had come into the writer's hands as a stray fragment from 14 another note of Paul. Alexander is probably to be identified with the man mentioned in 1 Tim. i. 20 as one of the two heretics who had been ' delivered up to Satan '—i.e. excommunicated—by Paul. If so, we have here a possible evidence that the Second Epistle to Timothy was written before the First, unless the writer inserted the fragment without noticing the contradiction involved in it. Instead of a heretic expelled from the Church, Alexander is here a troublesome member, against whom Timothy needs to be warned. An Alexander also comes before us in a puzzling passage of Acts (xix. 33), where it is doubtful whether he was a friend or an enemy of Paul. Since the Jews put him forward as their spokesman, it is probable that he was a Christian renegade, who was prepared to give evidence against his former teacher. If so, he may well be the man of whom Paul speaks resentfully in this verse. The epithet applied to him means literally a worker in brass or copper, but in later Greek was the general name for a smith. The mention of his trade was necessary, since Alexander was at this time one of the commonest of Greek names. Nothing is said as to the nature of the **harm** which Paul had suffered from Alexander. He may have spread some malicious gossip about the apostle, or got him into trouble with the civic authorities. More likely, he had tried to counteract Paul's teaching and won a number of followers ; this may be taken as certain if he was the Alexander of whom we hear in 1 Tim. i. 20. ' *The Lord will pay him back for what he has done* ' is a quotation of Psalm lxii. 12. Paul here obeys his own precept (Rom. xii. 19) that men must be content to leave all vengeance to God. This, however, would not be inconsistent with his excommunication of Alexander at a later time. A necessary act of Church discipline was on a different footing from the avenging of a personal offence. **Beware of him**—more 15 exactly : ' do you also beware of him.' We can gather that he was now in Timothy's neighbourhood, perhaps a newcomer to Ephesus, and likely to impose on Timothy by his plausible claim to be a zealous Christian. Paul warns his friend to be on his guard against the man, whose true character he had himself learned by hard experience. **He has been bitterly hostile to anything I have said** (lit. ' to our words '). Paul often uses ' we ' in place of ' I,' but in such cases he thinks of himself in his representative character as a servant of the Church. So he indicates here that his quarrel with Alexander was no mere personal one. This was a man who would be hostile to every missionary as he had been to Paul himself.

The Progress of the Trial (iv. 16–18)

16 The first time I had to defend myself, I had no supporters ;
everyone deserted me. (God grant it may not be brought
17 up against them !). But the Lord supported me and gave
me strength to make a full statement of the gospel, for all
the heathen to hear it, and I was rescued *from the jaws of*
18 *the lion*. The Lord will rescue me from every assault of
evil, He will bring me safe to His own realm in heaven. To
Him be glory for ever and ever ! Amen.

The passage presents a number of difficulties. Some of
them would be removed if we could assume that here also we
have part of a genuine letter, describing some conflict with the
authorities in which Paul was involved at an earlier stage of
his career. This would account for the tone of confidence
with which he speaks, and which is quite out of keeping with
the resignation to certain death in verses 6–8. We know that
he was in grave danger at Ephesus (2 Cor. i. 8–10), but on that
occasion his friends stood by him valiantly (Rom. xvi. 3, 4)
while he complains here that he was left quite alone. Possibly
he is describing the course of events after his arrest at Jerusalem. This would fit in with the reference to a 'first defence'
through which he had come successfully (Acts xxii. 30–xxiii.
11). It is significant that verse 17 of the present passage has an
exact parallel in Acts xxiii. 11 : ' The Lord stood by him, and
said, Be of good cheer, Paul.' Either the author of 2 Timothy
is quoting from the passage in Acts, or the author of Acts is
acquainted with some record similar to what is given here.

As the passage stands, it must be intended to describe the
Roman trial which Paul was now facing. When thus regarded
it may be explained in either of two ways : (1) Paul had been
tried at Rome and acquitted, and after an interval of perhaps a
year, during which he had carried on the work presupposed in
1 Timothy and Titus, he had been re-arrested. In the new
danger which confronts him he looks back on the earlier trial
and hopes for a similar outcome. (2) The reference is to one
trial, which fell into two parts. After a preliminary hearing in

which he had acquitted himself well, he had been remanded, and looks forward anxiously, but not without hope, to the next sitting of the court, at which his case would be decided. This is pretty certainly the situation which the writer means to suggest. He assumed that Timothy was still ignorant of the outcome of the first trial and needed to be informed. This would be absurd if Paul had since then been at freedom and had spent the time in missionary work, with Timothy as his companion.

The first time I had to defend myself must therefore mean 16 'at the first enquiry,' which was now to be followed by the more serious one. **I had no supporters, everyone deserted me.** If this was written by Paul himself after his arrest at Jerusalem, we may infer that the Jewish Christians, although they had welcomed him on his arrival (Acts xxi. 17) were unwilling to exert themselves on his behalf. From all that we know of their attitude to him, this may well have been. The writer, however, transfers the scene to Rome, where it was customary for a prisoner on trial to be accompanied by a number of friends, who attested by their presence that he was a man prized and respected. Paul, we are given to understand, had to face his ordeal without any of this moral support. By the interjected words ' may it not be laid to their charge,' a hint is given that his Roman friends had failed him through cowardice. Their failure is mentioned, however, in order to bring out the thought that Paul was not left alone. **But the Lord** 17 **supported me** (lit. ' stood by me ') **and gave me strength.** It is implied that by this Divine help he was enabled not merely to confront his judges, but to plead his cause successfully. Moffatt understands the next words to mean that before the Roman court Paul had courage **to make a full statement of the gospel,** and that in this way **all the heathen** heard it. Perhaps the meaning is more comprehensive. The words read literally, ' in order that through me the preaching might be accomplished.' Paul believed, as he tells us several times in his Epistles, that a commission had been laid on him to proclaim the gospel to the whole world. At the time of his trial this task was far from completion, but now he was encouraged to hope that he still might be able to carry it through. He had

been so sustained by Divine help that he might look forward
to acquittal. It was God's purpose that he should be restored
to liberty and finish his work—' that all the Gentiles might
hear the message.' This would seem to be the only natural
meaning of the words. When Paul speaks of ' all the Gentiles '
hearing him, he cannot very well imply that the judges on the
bench or the crowd that occupied the court-room were representative of the whole Gentile world. He is not concerned with
the trial itself, but with the result which he now hopes from it.
' I was rescued,' he goes on to say, ' *from the jaws of the lion.*'
This is a familiar Old Testament phrase for deliverance from
extreme danger, and we need not look for some covert allusion
to the emperor Nero, or to a possible death in the amphi-
theatre. The thought is simply that God, who on this occasion
18 has saved him, will continue His protection **and will rescue me
from every assault of evil.**

Some have found here an echo of the Lord's Prayer,
and the reference to a ' heavenly Kingdom,' together with
the closing doxology, also recalls the language of the
prayer. But these agreements are probably accidental.
Paul is not thinking, in the spirit of the Lord's Prayer, of
deliverance from moral evil, but of protection from the
malicious designs of men. He is certain not only of this
earthly protection, but of ultimate salvation : **the Lord will
bring me safe to His own realm in heaven.** It would be possible
to understand this hope in the light of such passages as 1 Thess.
iv. 15 and 1 Cor. xv. 51, where Paul expresses the confidence
that he would himself witness the Lord's return and pass alive
into the Kingdom. We know, however, that he latterly
abandoned this belief, and the verse, if written by Paul, must
date from this later period of his life. That he anticipated a
complete change in his condition—not the merging of his
present life in another, but the entrance into a new state of
being—is indicated in the emphatic word ' heavenly,' which
marks the contrast between the earthly scene of trouble and
suffering and the different world which awaits him after death.
It was the Jewish custom to add some expression of reverence

whenever the Divine name had been solemnly mentioned. So, after speaking of God's Kingdom, Paul says, **To Him be glory for ever and ever ! Amen.** This doxology serves the further purpose of bringing the Epistle to a close, for the remaining verses are of the nature of a postscript.

PERSONAL GREETINGS (iv. 19–22)

Salute Prisca and Aquila and the household of Onesiphorus. 19
    Erastus stayed on at Corinth : I left Trophimus ill at 20
    Miletus. Do your best to come before winter.   21
Eubulus salutes you ; so do Pudens, Linus, Claudia, and all the
    brotherhood.
The Lord Jesus be with your spirit.   22
Grace be with you.

    Salute Prisca and Aquila and the household of Onesiphorus. 19
It is noticeable that in this mention of the two most loyal of his helpers the wife is named before the husband—confirming the impression we get elsewhere that she was the more important of the two. It is significant, too, that they are assumed to be living at Ephesus, and had not returned to their former residence at Rome. The mention of them here lends support to the theory (very probable on other grounds) that Rom. xvi. does not properly belong to the Roman Epistle, but was originally a separate letter, addressed to the Church at Ephesus. The name of **Onesiphorus** has already occurred in a highly honourable connexion (i. 16–18). The conclusion that he was now dead is borne out by the greeting to his family and not to himself. **Erastus stayed on at Corinth.** This 20 friend of Paul is mentioned in Acts xix. 22, and also in Rom. xvi. 23, where he is described as ' steward of the city '—i.e. of Corinth. His name is coupled with that of Timothy in Acts xix. 22, and Timothy is here informed that his old comrade had stayed behind when Paul left Corinth. This would be natural if he was the city treasurer, though it is hard to see how his official duties had permitted him to act as one of Paul's assistants at Ephesus.

The notice of **Trophimus** involves several difficulties. We know from Acts that Trophimus was an Asian Christian, and one of the delegates who accompanied Paul to Jerusalem (Acts xx. 4). We should naturally assume that it was on this journey that he had fallen sick at Miletus ; but Paul would not have given the news of this sickness in a letter written six years afterwards. Moreover we hear again of Trophimus, in Acts xxi. 29, as seen in Paul's company at Jerusalem. If he had been left behind through sickness, he must speedily have recovered and caught up with Paul almost as soon as he reached his destination ; in this case there would have been no purpose in mentioning the brief illness at all, especially after the lapse of some years. It must be concluded either that the author of the Pastorals has strangely confused his facts, or that the reference is to some other journey than that of Acts xx. If 2 Timothy in its present form is genuine, it is necessary to assume that Paul had been liberated after a first trial, and had made a journey through Asia Minor which was still recent when he wrote. The more natural conjecture is that the verse belongs to some letter of Paul which has been 21 artificially attached to the present Epistle. **Do your best to come before winter.** This adds a note of urgency to the ' come quickly ' of verse 10. Any delay might involve a loss of months, owing to winter storms.

Greetings are now sent from friends who are with Paul as he writes, and from the Roman Church generally. There seems to be a contradiction with verse 11, where the apostle has said that he is alone except for Luke ; but he was there speaking of active workers, while he now refers simply to Christian friends. The names are all unknown, although legend has been busy with them, as with all names which are found in the 21 New Testament. **Linus,** according to the tradition of the Roman Church, was the immediate successor of Peter in the bishopric ; and it seems certain, from the testimony of Irenaeus and Eusebius, that there was a presbyter called Linus who at an early time was prominent at Rome. It is possible that the author of the Pastorals, in order to give a Roman colour to this letter, has thrown in the name of Linus, along with those of Pudens and Claudia, which also were Roman names. But all the names were in common use over the empire in the first century, and no special conclusions can be drawn from them.

The Epistle closes with the usual benediction. After the 22 individual blessing on Timothy there is a comprehensive one, ' Grace be with you all '—i.e. with the whole community to which Timothy belongs. This is strange at the end of a letter which is so intimately personal, and may help to confirm the view that in the closing chapter we have fragments of Paul's genuine correspondence. Or perhaps the author wished to convey a hint that the letter, while addressed to Timothy, is intended for all Christian workers.

THE EPISTLE OF PAUL TO TITUS

THE EPISTLE OF PAUL TO TITUS

SALUTATIONS (i. 1–4)

Paul a servant of God and an apostle of Jesus Christ for the 1
faith of God's elect and for their knowledge of the Truth
that goes with a religious life, serving in hope of the life 2
eternal which God, who never lies, promised ages ago—
He gave effect to His word in due time by a proclamation 3
with which I have been entrusted by command of God our
Saviour ;—to Titus my lawful son in the faith we hold in 4
common ; grace and peace from God the Father and Christ
Jesus our Saviour.

The salutation is unduly drawn out for a brief letter, and
is so complicated in structure that the thought is difficult to
follow. This may be partly due to the writer's effort to crowd
in a large number of Pauline ideas, and partly to his anxiety
that in a letter which will be mainly practical the religious
basis of the Christian life should not be forgotten. At the
outset, therefore, under cover of the salutation, he lays
emphasis on what he conceives to be the fundamental Christian
beliefs.

Paul describes himself constantly, in the genuine Epistles,
as a 'servant of Christ'; here he is a servant of God and an 1
apostle of Jesus Christ. This is probably meant to bring into
clear relief the distinctive nature of the gospel. The ancient
prophets were 'servants of God,' but Paul, while he was their
successor, was also entrusted with the new message which
God had given through Christ. This idea of a new revelation
pervades the passage that follows. He is an apostle for the
faith of God's elect. The Greek would naturally mean ' according to the faith.' This translation is rejected by many scholars
since it would describe the message of Paul as in some way
regulated by the faith of others, instead of forming and

directing it. But the difficulty disappears when we think of the writer as drawing a contrast between the old and the new types of faith. Paul's work as an apostle is in keeping with the new revelation to which the elect have responded. This thought is made more explicit : ' **and according to their knowledge of the Truth that goes with a religious life.'** Paul's teaching agrees with that new knowledge which has come to Christians through the gospel, and which finds its expression in the 2 Christian way of life. The Christian, however, looks forward to a life to come. His earthly service is grounded in this immortal **hope,** and derives from it all that makes it Christian. Paul can thus speak of his apostleship as conditioned by that knowledge of the Truth which goes hand in hand with ' godliness ' or ' piety,' a present life with God which is bound up with the life hereafter. This, on the whole, seems the best interpretation of a condensed and loosely constructed sentence. Moffatt would connect the words **in hope of life eternal** with Paul's reference to himself as a servant of God and an apostle. This may be the meaning ; but throughout the Epistles it is the Christian life generally which is associated with the future life. To make the immortal hope merely the ground of Paul's apostleship seems to narrow the thought unduly.

The life to which Christians look forward is one **which God, who never lies, promised ages ago** (lit. ' before endless ages '). This might denote ' before time began.' Yet it is plain from the context that the allusion is not to God's eternal plan, but to a promise which He made in the distant past. Strictly speaking, there is no doctrine of immortality in the Old Testament, but the writer is justified in claiming that the idea of a higher life lies at the heart of Scripture. Before the coming of Christ the promise had seemed baseless ; but God cannot be 3 untrue to His word (cf. Rom. iii. 4). **In due time**—i.e. at the time which He Himself had appointed—He ' manifested ' the life ; in Christ He gave the visible pledge of the immortality which men had known hitherto through the veiled promises.

By an abrupt turn the life now changes into the message concerning it. **He gave effect to His word by a proclamation with which I have been entrusted.** The life was brought to light by the Christian message, and was in some manner inherent in the message. Jesus can say in the Fourth Gospel, ' the words which I speak to you are life ' (John vi. 63), since by faith in the message the life is imparted. With this life-giving message Paul was entrusted **by command of God our Saviour.** In Paul's other letters the commission is regarded as given by Christ (cf. Gal. i. 12: 'I received it by the revelation of Jesus Christ'), but here it is referred directly to God, since it deals with the life which God Himself has promised. This explains, also, why God is spoken of as **our Saviour,** the God who had purposed from the beginning to save His elect people. Paul's apostleship is thus linked up with the Divine plan. God, who had designed and effected the salvation, had also appointed Paul to proclaim it. After the long digression the greeting is now completed : **to Titus my lawful son in a faith we hold in** 4 **common.** Paul thought of all his converts as his children (Gal. iv. 19 ; 1 Cor. iv. 14-15), but in Titus he recognizes a son who inherits his faith. Titus is, in the fullest sense, the son of his father.

There is no mention of Titus in the book of Acts, but he takes a prominent place in two of Paul's Epistles. It was he whom Paul took with him to the Council of Jerusalem (Gal. ii. 3) as his proof case that a Gentile might be truly a Christian without circumcision. He alludes to him a number of times in 2 Corinthians as his intermediary with the Church at Corinth in days when it was vacillating in its allegiance. Again and again in that Epistle Paul alludes to him as one whom he entirely trusted and who ' walked in the same spirit ' (2 Cor. xii. 18 ; ii. 3 ; viii. 23). It was his arrival with the good news that the Corinthian Church was reconciled which caused Paul immediately to write the beautiful Second Epistle, expressing a joy he could hardly contain. There is good reason to believe that Titus was himself largely responsible for bringing about this happy reconciliation. He was evidently a favourite at Corinth (2 Cor. xii. 17-18), and seems to have been a man of tact and wisdom—better fitted, perhaps, than Paul himself to handle a delicate situation. It may have been Paul's own allusions to Titus which suggested him to the author of the

Pastorals as the confidential assistant to whom Paul might address a letter of this kind. It may also be conjectured that when these Epistles were written the memory of Titus was still fresh in the Church. Among other things it would be known that Titus had worked in Crete, and this letter is supposed to reach him while he was engaged in that mission.

The greeting at last closes, as it opened, with the names of God and Christ entwined together. It can hardly be a matter of accident that the title **our Saviour** which has just been applied to God is now transferred to Christ. Perhaps the object is to make clear that, while it is ultimately God who saves, He yet effects His purpose through Christ. It will be noticed, too, that the word **Saviour** is used in two different senses. As applied to God, it has the vaguer, Old Testament meaning of a God who helps and delivers. When used of Christ, it acquires a more specific significance. It was Christ who performed the great saving act for mankind, and who therefore bears the title of ' Saviour ' as part of His proper name. The title does not occur in the earlier New Testament books, and was probably borrowed from Hellenistic religion, where it is the common epithet of divinities who free their worshippers from the bondage of the earthly life.

THE CHOICE OF ELDERS (i. 5–9)

5 I left you behind in Crete in order to finish putting things right and also to appoint presbyters in every town as I told

6 you, men who are above reproach, only once married, with children who believe and who are not liable to the

7 charge of being profligate or insubordinate. [For a bishop must be above reproach—he is a steward of God's house— he must not be presumptuous or hot-tempered or a

8 drunkard or violent or addicted to pilfering ; he must be hospitable, a lover of goodness, master of himself, a just

9 man, a religious man, and abstemious ; he must hold by

the sure truths of doctrine so as to be able to give instruction in sound doctrine and refute objections raised by
any.]¹

After the salutation the Epistle at once takes on a practical
character. Titus is reminded of the task to which Paul has
appointed him, and receives additional counsels as to how he
should perform it. His first business is to see that the management of the Church is placed in competent hands.

I left you behind in Crete. It is here implied that Paul him-   5
self had been in Crete with Titus, and had left him to complete a
work in which they had been engaged together. We are thus
confronted at the outset with the question which throws
doubt on the authenticity of the Epistle. When did Paul
labour in Crete ? It has been shown in the Introduction that
Paul never indicates in his other Epistles that he had visited
the island, and that the book of Acts only mentions the occasion when he had touched it casually, as a prisoner on the ship
for Rome. No place can be found for a mission to Crete within
the known framework of Paul's life ; if he worked there it must
have been in the hypothetical period after his Roman imprisonment. The Epistle assumes that Titus had been left in Crete
to finish putting things right (lit. ' to arrange the matters remaining over '). Paul himself had laid down the general lines
of the mission, and had left Titus in charge to adjust the
details. To assist him in this work (which is often the most
troublesome part of a big enterprise), Paul writes him this
letter. The first duty is to appoint presbyters in every town.
It is assumed in 1 Timothy that government by elders is
already in existence : Titus is here conceived as establishing it
for the first time. This would imply that Crete was newly
evangelized and as yet had no settled Church order ; although
the reference to **every town** would suggest that Christianity
had now spread over the whole of the large island. Perhaps the
emphasis is to be laid on the next words : **as I told you.** Titus
is to see to it not so much that elders are appointed as that

¹ This passage seems to have been added, rather awkwardly, to the
original text.

Paul's instructions in this respect are duly carried out. The pronoun I is made emphatic, but not for the purpose of distinguishing the methods of Paul from others which are to be avoided ; nothing more is indicated than that the institution of elders was approved by Paul, who himself laid down the rules which were henceforth to be followed.

A question has been raised as to whether Titus is here authorized to appoint elders, without any co-operation on the part of the Church. Perhaps it is assumed that, since the Cretan communities had newly come into being, the missionary himself had to furnish them with officers, as Paul and Barnabas had done in Asia Minor, on their first journey (Acts xiv. 23 : ' they ordained elders in every church '). Or the meaning may be simply that Titus is to order the necessary elections, or to confirm the appointments made by them. In any case we have here one of a number of evidences that these Epistles were not intended to supply a code for Church procedure. In any such code precise regulations would be given as to how the elections should be made. Everything of this kind is here passed over, and the directions deal only with the character of the men elected.

6 They must be men **above reproach, only once married.** As in I Tim. iii. 3, nothing more seems to be intended than that the elders must have been faithful in the marriage relation. Sometimes it has been inferred that none but married men should be chosen ; but it might equally well be argued from the next words that the elder must have children. It is taken for granted in both cases that the elders, as men of mature age, would be heads of families ; and the whole object is to secure that the officers of the Church should be of good moral character, and serve in their own persons as examples to the Church. As they are Christian men themselves, they are to have ' faithful children '—i.e. **children who believe.** In the parallel passage, I Tim. iii. 4, the elder is required to have his children under proper control, and it has been held that the word ' faithful ' ought here also to be understood in the sense of ' loyal ' or ' dutiful.' But in view of the general New Testament usage the meaning is almost certainly that the elder's

children must be Christians, and worthy of the name—not liable to the charge of being profligate or insubordinate. The children are evidently thought of as grown up, and now proving by their conduct that they had come out of a Christian home. All this has a significant bearing on the origin of the Epistle. Inadvertently the writer lets us know that he belongs to a second Christian generation, and that he is not Paul making rules for a Church which has newly been founded.

The reasons why none but exemplary men should be chosen are now given. They follow the general lines of I Tim. iii. 2f., but there is no ground for assuming that they have been intruded from the other Epistle into this one. They are by no means literally repeated, and without them the account of what an elder should be would not be adequate. **For a bishop 7 must be above reproach,** as being a steward of God's house. In an ordinary household the most trusty servant was chosen as steward, and the same rule must obtain in the household of God. The verse is conclusive proof that in the Pastorals ' elder ' and ' bishop ' mean the same thing, for it is clear that the man now described as bishop is the same as the elder of the preceding verse. No doubt the alternative name is now given him because of its literal meaning of ' overseer,' which itself indicates the duty of a steward. **Above reproach** is vague, and Titus is therefore told what is involved in it—**not presumptuous or hot-tempered,** for such a disposition is not only foreign to the best type of character, but unfits a man for the work of governing others. **Not a drunkard or violent** (lit. ' a striker,' and perhaps this meaning is implied ; with passionate southern temperaments, angry words soon pass to blows, and stress is laid in these Epistles on the dignity as well as the virtue which should mark a Christian officer. A man who might involve himself in a street brawl would soon bring the Church into disrespect.) **Not addicted to pilfering** (lit. ' to making base gains '). In later Church orders—e.g. that of Hippolytus—this was taken to mean that men of certain occupations were excluded, and a number of trades were specified which automatically barred a man from Church office. But the writer is evidently thinking (as in I Tim.) of moral qualities, and places his ban on men of a sordid and miserly disposition. This perhaps is more in his mind than actual stealing, which an elder would hardly be guilty of, even in Crete.

8 The positive qualities which are necessary are now enumerated : hospitable, a lover of goodness, master of himself, a just man, a religious man, and abstemious. There is no reason to look for any special motive in the selection or arrangement of these virtues. They are put down almost at random, in order to convey a general idea of the type of man who ought to be chosen as an elder. He must be a kindly, sensible, honest, clean-living man. No demand is made for any rare qualities, moral or religious. The writer has in his mind an average Christian community and the worthy, capable men who are sure to be found in it. Out of the best material that lies to his hand Titus must choose his elders. One qualification,
9 however, is essential : the elder must hold by the sure truths of doctrine, as opposed to those false teachings which are presently to be dealt with. As a leader in the Church he must represent its genuine beliefs ; he must not only hold to them himself, but must be able to give instruction in sound doctrine and confute those who oppose it. The ability to teach is here made one of the requirements of a good elder, although in I Tim. v. 17 the elder who has this gift is spoken of as exceptional and entitled to special honour. This difference may be a sign that the Epistle to Titus belongs to a later date, when more was demanded of an elder ; or it may point to an earlier date, before Church offices had been fully differentiated, and an elder was expected to turn his hand to anything ; or it may only mean that this Epistle was intended for a given locality, where the danger from heresy was acute and all Church leaders had to be capable of meeting it. This would seem to be implied in the following passage, in which Crete is described as a hot-bed of false teaching.

THE HERETICS AND THEIR DOCTRINES (i. 10–16)

10 For there are plenty of insubordinate creatures who impose on people with their empty arguments, particularly those who

have come over from Judaism ; they must be silenced, for 11 they are undermining whole families by teaching objectionable doctrine for the base end of making money. It has 12 been said by one of themselves, by a prophet of their own, that—

' Cretans are always liars, evil beasts, lazy gluttons.'

That is a true statement. So deal sharply with them, to 13 have them sound in the faith instead of studying Jewish 14 myths and rules laid down by men who discard the Truth. For the pure all things are pure, but nothing is pure for 15 the polluted and unbelieving ; their very mind and conscience are polluted ; they profess to know God, but they 16 deny Him by their deeds ; they are detestable, disobedient, and useless for good work of any kind.

The heresies in Crete were apparently of much the same nature as those condemned in 1 and 2 Timothy ; and much the same language is applied to them. More stress, however, is laid on their Jewish characteristics, which were only hinted at in the other Epistles (cf. 1 Tim. i. 7f. ; iv. 7 ; vi. 4 ; 2 Tim. iii. 6 ; iv. 4). Moreover, the heresies are brought into close relation with general conditions in the island of Crete. This may only belong to the dramatic setting of the Epistle ; Titus is supposed to be working in Crete, and a few references to the well-known character of its people may be thrown in by way of local colour. Much more probably there is some real connexion between this Epistle and Crete. It can hardly have been intended for the Cretan Churches, for, even if the writer had wished to rebuke his readers, he would not have gone to work by insulting their country, as he does here. It may be conjectured that he had in view some type of error which had originated in Crete or was especially prevalent in that island, and against which he feels it necessary to warn the other Churches.

The passage takes up the reference to ' adversaries ' which closed the previous section—a further proof that verses 7–9 are integral to the Epistle. **For there are plenty of insubordinate** 10 **creatures.** The construction is ambiguous, but it seems better to translate, 'For they (i.e. the adversaries) are many—insubordinate, empty chatterers, deceivers.' Three charges are brought against them. They are disloyal to the Church and its doctrines ; their teaching consists of nothing but sounding words ; they impose on their hearers and on themselves. These are only the general invectives which are employed in theological controversies of all ages, and nothing is told us of the real nature of the teaching in question. That it had some relation to Judaism is evident from the words that follow : **particularly those who have come over from Judaism.** From this it can be gathered that both Jews and Gentiles were among the false teachers, but that the Jewish members of the group held the erroneous views in a more pronounced or obnoxious form. We are reminded of the heresy attacked in Colossians, in which pagan and Jewish ideas seem to have been mixed up together ; but the Colossian heresy is itself obscure, and it would be hazardous to assume that the one denounced here was identical with it. Gnosticism as it comes before us in the second century was strongly anti-Jewish, but this was probably a later development. In the earlier phases of Christian gnosticism there was doubtless a tendency to combine Jewish practices and beliefs with borrowings from paganism, and this mingled type of doctrine would exist under many forms.

11   The disturbers of the Church **must be silenced.** A word is used which means literally ' put something on the mouth,' and can apply either to a bridle or a muzzle. If taken in the former sense, it would enjoin that those unruly persons must be brought under proper control. Perhaps the other sense is preferable, and would fit in with the reference to ' vicious animals ' in the next verse. In any case, these perverters of the gospel must be silenced, but nothing is said of expelling them from the Church. They are simply to be kept within bounds, **for they are undermining whole families by teaching objectionable doctrine for the base end of making money.** We learn from 2 Tim. iii. 6 that they worked through individuals—chiefly thoughtless women—and the point of this verse is that by their influence over one or two of its members they brought dissension and misery on the whole household. The motive

of it all was the desire for money—referring either to the fees they took for their tuition, or to the gifts they expected from ardent disciples. Several times in the Pastorals the heretical teachers are charged with mercenary motives, and we need not doubt that among them there were mere impostors, as among modern spiritualists and faith-healers. But the later gnostic movement certainly included some of the most earnest spirits of the Church, and this would also be true of the heresy in its earlier stages.

It has been said by one of themselves, a prophet of their own. 12 The allusion is to Epimenides, a Cretan, who lived about 500 B.C., and who was numbered among the seven wise men of Greece. In his own lifetime he was credited with supernatural insight, and was once invited to Athens to advise the city as to the sacrifices necessary to stay a plague. On his instruction an altar was raised ' to an unknown God,' and there is therefore a twofold link between this heathen sage and the New Testament. Long after his death Epimenides was held in reverence as a prophet, and is so mentioned by Aristotle, Cicero, and other ancient writers. He is said to have foretold the Persian war ten years before it happened, and predictions attributed to him were widely current, like those of Thomas the Rhymer and Michael Scott. The author of the Pastorals quotes him in his known character as a prophet. Whether he considered this wise heathen to have been divinely inspired is beside the point. He merely says, ' Here was a man whom the Cretans themselves regard as a prophet.' It is doubtful whether Epimenides himself wrote the hexameter line which follows, although several writers shortly after the Christian era assign it definitely to a poem of his ' Concerning Oracles,' and the first part of it appears (evidently as a quotation) in some verses by Callimachus (about 270 B.C.). Cretans are always liars, evil beasts, lazy gluttons. How the Cretans, more than other Greeks, won their reputation for lying, we do not know ; but the idea was so general that it came to be embodied in the word ' to Cretize ' —i.e. to lie. One of the famous puzzles in Greek logic was based on the line before us : ' Since a Cretan said that all Cretans are liars, must it not follow that they speak the truth ? Yet this cannot be, if a Cretan lied.' The rest of the line describes the people as treacherous and brutish, lazy and greedy. If Epimenides wrote the line, it was no doubt at a moment when he thought himself badly used by his countrymen, but there was just enough truth in his criticism to make it generally accepted. The Cretans were islanders, living for the most part under primitive conditions when the rest of the Greeks had passed on to a higher stage of culture. They gave the impression of an uncouth, half-barbarous race, although archaeology has now taught us that Crete had attained to a high civilization many centuries before Greece itself.

To the unflattering testimony of the Cretan prophet the
13 writer adds that is a true statement. Perhaps he merely echoes the popular opinion, but more likely he speaks from some unfortunate personal experience, or from his knowledge of the Church's difficulties in Crete. All through the Epistle one has the impression that it has a special bearing on Cretan circumstances. **So deal sharply with them.** Since the Cretans are naturally so boorish and cantankerous, little can be done with them by mild persuasion. They must be spoken to in plain terms, if the rebuke is to have any effect. At the same time there is no suggestion of excommunicating the evildoers (as in 1 Tim. i. 20) ; Titus is to play the part of a stern physician rather than of a judge, **to make them sound in the faith.** Elsewhere the true faith is itself described as ' healthy,' in contrast to the perversions of heresy ; the idea of sickness is here trans-
14 ferred to the victims of heretical teaching, **who study Jewish myths and rules of men who have disowned the Truth.** The ' myths ' are doubtless the same as the ' old wives' fables ' of 1 Tim. i. 3. They are now expressly called Jewish, and may be identified with those legends embroidered on the Old Testament history in which the more esoteric ideas of Judaism were often conveyed. This is confirmed by the further reference to ' commandments of men,' a phrase of Isaiah (xxix. 13) which Jesus Himself applies to the scribal tradition with which the Law had been overlaid (Mark vii. 7). These new **rules or commandments have been devised, not only by men, but by men who discard the Truth**—i.e. the true gospel.

From the verses which follow we can gather that the man-made ' commandments ' were of the nature indicated in 1 Tim. iv. 3–6—prohibitions imposed on marriage and on certain meats and drinks. **For the pure all things are pure.** The idea 15 may be partly supplied by the saying of Jesus in Luke xi. 41 (' Behold, all things are clean to you '), and by Paul's declaration in Rom. xiv. 20 (' All things are indeed pure '). But it has parallels in Greek and Roman literature, and the writer may be quoting a current proverb. His meaning is that ritual purity is at best artificial. Nothing really counts except the clean heart, and to those who have it all the distinctions of clean and unclean are meaningless. The phrase has passed into our common language, in the sense that those who are themselves pure are unaffected by impure things—a sentiment which is often very dubious. Here the writer is thinking along ritual rather than moral lines. There is something in inward purity which cleanses everything, so that ceremonial rules cease to have any value. On the other hand **nothing is pure for the polluted and unbelieving.** This last word usually denotes non-Christians, but here it must almost certainly be taken in the wider sense of ' irreligious,' devoid of any feeling for God. **Their very mind and conscience are polluted.** They look at all things from a wholly material point of view, and for such men it is not merely things ritually forbidden which defile. Everything in God's world partakes of the unhallowed quality which is inherent in their own minds. That the writer is not thinking of ' unbelievers ' in any technical sense, is clear from the next verse. The men he has in mind, men of coarse, earthly temper, are often nominally Christian. **They profess 16 to know God, but deny Him by their deeds.** It is not necessary to explain this with reference to the false teachers and their victims. Thinking of them, the writer has been led to speak generally of all who make profession of religion but who have never really known what it means. Practice is the only confession of faith which has any value. There can be no real knowledge of God in men who are **detestable, disobedient, and useless for good work of any kind.** In the first word there is a reminiscence of the Old Testament phrase ' abomination to the

Lord,' applied in the book of Proverbs to various evil practices of which the men here in question have been guilty. The 'man of God' is described in 2 Tim. iii. 17 as 'fully equipped for every good work'; contrasted with him is the 'unbeliever,' who for every good work is useless. The word means literally 'counterfeit,' and is perhaps to be understood in this sense. Men who make loud professions are often found to be base metal when tested by their deeds.

DUTIES OF VARIOUS GROUPS (ii. 1–10)

ii.

1-2 You must instruct people in what is due to sound doctrine. Tell the older men to be temperate, serious, masters of them-

3 selves, sound in faith, in love, and in stedfastness. Tell the older women also to be reverent in their demeanour and

4 not to be slanderers or slaves to drink; they must give good counsel, so that the young women may be trained to

5 love their husbands and children, to be mistress of themselves, chaste, domestic, kind, and submissive to their husbands—otherwise it will be a scandal to the gospel.

6 Tell the young men also to be masters of themselves at all

7 points; set them an example of good conduct; be sincere

8 and serious in your teaching, let your words be sound and such that no exception can be taken to them, so that the opposite side may be confounded by finding nothing that

9 they can say to our discredit. Tell servants to be submissive to their masters and to give them satisfaction all round,

10 not to be refractory, not to embezzle, but to prove themselves truly faithful at all points, so as to be an ornament to the doctrine of God our Saviour in all respects.

Titus has been enjoined to choose the elders carefully, since the welfare of the whole community depends on them. But all the members of the Church must do their part. Each group of them must receive the appropriate teaching and example, so that all may further the cause of the gospel. There is little in the chapter which has not already found a place in 1 Timothy, but the earlier instructions are not merely repeated ; they are presented, in each case, from some fresh point of view, and are brought together in a single continuous passage, which makes clear to us, more perhaps than any other, the real interest in these Epistles. The writer is concerned throughout not so much with matters of Church order as with the preservation of Christian standards. He feels that the Church will fail in its purpose unless all its various members have learned a new way of life, based on religious principles. The account of the Cretans in the previous chapter gives the more weight to this demand for Christian living. Crete is the example of a community which is not merely pagan, but on a low level of even pagan morals. It is shown how such a community may be transformed by a discipline in the Christian rule of life.

You must instruct people in what is due to sound doctrine. 1 The ' you ' is emphatic. Since others have been misleading the Cretans, Titus must be the more earnest in his own duty. A double contrast is understood in this verse. The moral atmosphere of Crete itself is tainted, and even the Church in Crete has been influenced for the worse by false teachers. Against all these evil forces Titus must insist on a mode of living which is in keeping with the gospel. **He is to tell the** 2 **older men to be temperate, serious, masters of themselves.** Even in their outward behaviour they must observe the gravity which is suitable to old age, and to the ordinary virtues they must add the specifically Christian ones : they **must be sound in faith, in love, and in stedfastness.** As the Christian teaching is itself ' healthy,' they must practise it in a healthy manner. For Paul the cardinal Christian virtues are faith, hope, and love. The writer of the Pastorals here substitutes ' patience ' or **stedfastness** for hope. Perhaps he thinks of hope as included in the faith which lays hold of the life to come. Or perhaps he sets patience in the place of hope because he is thinking specially of old men, whose attitude to life is now one of resignation.

Tell the older women also to be reverent in their demeanour. 3 An expressive word, **reverent,** is used, which properly denotes a priestess engaged in her duties ; the aged Christian woman is to carry about with her an atmosphere of religion, and this should be apparent in her look and action. The word **demeanour** might be taken in a narrower sense as ' dress,' and the writer doubtless means this to be included. But it is evident from the context that he is thinking of the impression which is made by the whole bearing and appearance of a good Christian woman as she grows old. **Not slanderers or slaves to drink**—like a familiar type of worldly woman, whose interests finally become confined to malicious gossip and the pampering of her own body. The coupling of slander and wine-drinking is significant. In ancient times, when wine was the only beverage, it was at their little wine-parties that old women would tear their neighbours' characters to pieces. **They must give good counsel** (expressed in Greek by a single word, ' nobly-teaching '). No formal instruction is implied, and perhaps no instruction put into words. The older women were to stand out in their own persons as patterns of a good life. It would naturally be on other women that their example

4 would chiefly tell, **so that the young women may be trained to love their husbands and children**—i.e. to attend to their home

5 duties instead of wasting themselves in frivolities. **Mistress of themselves** ; we have here that word for prudence or self-control which meets us constantly in these Epistles. As applied more particularly to women it denotes good temper, practical wisdom, strict conscientiousness. The two words **domestic, kind** may possibly go together in the sense of ' good house-workers ' (or, according to another reading, ' good house-keepers '). But when they are separated, as in our translation, they give a fine and suggestive meaning instead of a common-place one. Although assiduous in household tasks, the women are not to be wrapped up in them. They must be careful to preserve the larger sympathies which the too active housewife is so apt to lose. **Submissive to their husbands—otherwise it will be a scandal to the gospel.** An interesting sidelight is here thrown on the difficulties of the Early Church. Under the influence of Christian ideas of liberty women were claiming emancipation, in a manner that often clashed with ancient

notions of fitness and decorum. The writer is aware that the aggressiveness of many of its women was one of the hindrances to the work of the Church. The Christian message itself was too often misunderstood because it seemed to produce women of a wilful, domineering type.

The **young men** are likewise to be taught **to be masters of 6 themselves at all points.** Here again a primary place is given to the self-control which ranked, in Greek ethics, with justice, wisdom, and courage. There is truth in the view that in the teaching of the Pastorals the higher pagan morality is combined with the Christian, and sometimes tends to displace it. At the same time the ' self-mastery ' required is different from that of the pagan moralists. In some respects it answers to the humility on which emphasis is laid in the Gospels. Christians are to realize that they are servants of God, and must subdue their own will and passions in order to serve Him better. The moral virtue becomes also a religious one, as comes out clearly in the sequel to the present verse. **Set them an 7 example of good conduct ;** Titus is not only to give good counsel to others, but must illustrate his teaching by his own life. The injunction has a special fitness in its present place, for Titus, like Timothy (1 Tim. iv. 12), is himself a young man. But the precept to set an example is plainly meant to cover all the previous part of the chapter. All classes of men and women are to find in Titus himself something which they can imitate. He must be not only a pattern of well-doing, but sincere and serious in his teaching. On the one hand he is to show absolute sincerity (lit. ' incorruption ') of motive, in contrast to the self-seeking of the false teachers. On the other hand his teaching must be marked by a ' dignity,' an elevation of thought and language and manner, in keeping with its theme. **Let your words be sound.** In its substance, as in its motive 8 and form, his teaching must be ' healthy,' free from everything to which exception might be taken, **so that the opposite side may be confounded.** A vague term is purposely used to include all who are opposed to Titus in his work—the heathen critic as well as the heretic within the Church. All adversaries are to be silenced **by finding nothing that they can say to our**

discredit. Titus is to remember that he is the official spokesman of the Church, and that the world will judge it from what he does and teaches. In this verse we again have the positive note which is characteristic of the Epistles. Although they are largely concerned with heathen opposition and heretical doctrine, they studiously avoid all controversy. The writer puts his faith in the self-evident truth of the Christian message. He believes that all critics will be answered if it is only presented as it really is.

As in I Tim. vi. I, a transition is now made to the slave members of the Church, who were not free like the others to determine their own manner of life, and for whom separate 9 counsels were therefore necessary. **Tell servants to be submissive to their masters and to give them satisfaction all round** (lit. ' in all things to be obliging '). This advice was called in question, even in ancient times, on the ground that there were some things in which a Christian slave could not, and must not, obey a heathen master. But it may be that the advice was only intended for slaves who formed part of a Christian household. They were apt, as we know from I Tim. vi. 2, to abuse their privilege of being treated as brethren, and a warning is here given against undue presumption. They are **not to be** 10 **refractory** (lit. ' speak back again '), **not to embezzle, but to prove themselves truly faithful.** All these cautions would seem to be aimed at slaves who took advantage of their favoured position in a Christian family. The word translated ' embezzle ' means literally ' keep separate,' and is sometimes used in the sense of being underhand or secretive. But in its present connexion it is almost certainly a euphemism for stealing. **So as to be an ornament to the doctrine of God our Saviour in all respects.** The slave is reminded that in his lowly office he may do service for God, and this knowledge that he is working for the honour of the gospel is to safeguard his self-respect. The Christian message is called ' the teaching of God our Saviour ' in order to prepare the way for the next section, in which it is to be described as God's revelation to the world.

The Religious Basis of Christian Action (ii. 11-15)

For the grace of God has appeared to save all men, and it schools 11-
us to renounce irreligion and worldly passions and to live a 12
life of self-mastery, of integrity, and of godliness in this
present world, awaiting the blessed hope of the appearance 13
of the Glory of the great God and of our Saviour Christ
Jesus, who gave Himself up for us to redeem us from all 14
iniquity and secure Himself a clean people with a zest for
good deeds.
Tell them all this, exhort and reprove them with full authority ; 15
let no one slight you.

This fine section, which constitutes the heart of the Epistle,
is immediately connected with the admonition to slaves. But
it is evidently meant to explain all that has gone before and
is to follow. Directions have been given for life in a Christian
community, and it is now shown that the new rule of conduct
has its ground in the nature of the Christian message. A
revelation of God's mercy has been given through Christ, and
all to whom it comes will realize the debt which they owe to
God and which they are bound to discharge by a life conform-
able to His will.

For the grace of God has appeared to save all men. Mention 11
has just been made of ' God our Saviour,' and this name, as
used in the Old Testament, simply meant the God who
shields and delivers. But for the Christian it has acquired a
grander and more definite meaning : God has revealed a grace
which is intended to save all mankind. The two words ' grace '
and ' revealed ' are both emphatic. Other attributes of God
might be inferred from His visible action in nature and in
human history, but His grace, the free goodness whereby He
intervened for man's salvation, could never have been sur-
mised. It appeared, like a great light suddenly arising. Elsewhere in the Epistles the ' appearance ' of Christ is His coming
to earth, or His future coming in glory. Here the word is used
to denote the whole Christian message, as conveyed through
the life and death of Christ and everything He had taught.

This all constituted a single revelation of God's grace, which was intended to save the whole human family, not merely some favoured race or class. In order to effect its purpose, the 12 grace **schools** or 'educates' us in our several duties. A thought is here conveyed which may almost be taken as the key to the teaching of the Pastorals, and which distinguishes it from that of Paul. For Paul the grace of God consists in a single overwhelming gift which is received in a moment by the act of faith. In the Pastorals it is conceived as working continuously through a steady persistence in Christian belief and practice. Conversion is only an initial step, like a child's mastery of the alphabet. It makes possible the 'education' which is carried on through the whole of life and forms the convert into a true servant of Christ. In all this education the grace of God keeps working, like a ripening sun, by means of all the influences of Christian teaching and example.

This idea of education by grace is now defined and expanded : **to renounce irreligion and worldly passions.** The action of grace is on the one hand negative, leading men to give up their former indifference to God and their earth-bound desires, and **to live a life of self-mastery, of integrity and of godliness** (or, piety). The three words describe man's life in its threefold relation—to himself, to his fellow-men, and to God. He must learn to control his own passions, to deal justly with his neighbours, to worship God and obey Him. Man's own effort may be so assisted by the Divine power that in all these relations he may live worthily **in this present world.** It is implied that we are now subject to conditions in which the true life is not fully possible. According to the Jewish belief which passed over into Christianity, the 'present age' is under the dominion of evil powers, which will be overthrown when God brings in His Kingdom. Christians look forward to that coming age, and even now, amidst the surrounding evil, God's grace is training them for it, through the exercise of self-control, justice, 13 and piety. The writer thus thinks of Christians as **awaiting the blessed hope.** As frequently in the New Testament, **hope** here means the thing hoped for, the supreme event to which Christian faith and longing are directed. It will take the form of an appearance of the Glory of the great God and of our Saviour Christ Jesus. The term which was used in verse 11 for God's whole revelation is now applied to the final advent of Christ, who will ' appear ' in glory to judge the world and establish the promised Kingdom.

This hope of the Parousia had been the sustaining motive of earlier Christianity ; it had now receded into a distant future, and the Church had settled down to an indefinite period of waiting, in which the grace of God would continue its educative work. Yet the hope still hovered before the minds of Christians as the goal towards which they were striving, and the writer is able to speak of it in the language familiar to the previous generation. In one respect, however, he might seem to introduce a momentous change. His words are capable of the translation, ' the appearance of our great God and Saviour, Jesus Christ.' From a strictly linguistic point of view this is the more natural rendering, and it would require us to assume that for this writer Christ was now completely identified with God. It may be argued, however, that the identification is made nowhere else in the Epistles, and is not even suggested. Moreover, in the present passage the writer is concerned with one of the fixed beliefs of the Church, and his statement of it cannot be essentially different from the others which have come down to us. Wherever the Parousia is mentioned in the New Testament or the early Christian literature, it is taken for granted that the Messiah who comes in the clouds of heaven is distinct from God. He comes in the power of God, accompanied by angels, but He is the representative of God, not God Himself. So it is best to understand the verse as in Moffatt's translation. Believers look for the appearing of a glory which is at once that of God and of Christ, or rather, it is the Glory of God with which Christ is invested at His coming. The writer expresses in his own manner the normal apocalyptic expectation that ' the Son of man will come in the glory of the Father with His angels ' (Matt. xvi. 27).

One peculiarity of the verse is the epithet great, at first sight meaningless and superfluous when applied to

God. Some have found in it an evidence that Christ is described as God, not the absolute God, but a Divine being of exalted rank. More likely the meaning is that the full effulgence of Divine glory will surround Christ at His coming. The idea of greatness belongs to the glory, although it is transferred to God, from whom the glory emanates. That Christ is thought of as distinct from God seems to be evident from the
14 allusion which follows to the work which Christ had accomplished : **who gave Himself up for us to redeem us from all iniquity.** Since He died for the very purpose of delivering us, we can await His coming with entire confidence ; He will return to rescue finally from all the powers of evil those whom He has already set free. At the same time the verse is meant to connect the thought of Christ's future coming with that of the Divine grace now operating. By that grace we are enabled to live for God, in spite of present evils, and it will perfect its work when this age gives place to the Kingdom of God. Christians will inherit that Kingdom, since Christ came **to secure Himself a clean people** (lit. ' to purify for Himself a peculiar people '). The idea of consecration is here combined with that of cleansing from all defilement. Christ gave Himself in order that He might set apart for God those who believe in Him. The sacrificial conception of the death of Christ which is so prominent in the Epistle to the Hebrews is absent from the Pastorals, but here we may discern at least a suggestion of it. The term which describes the Church as consecrated is taken over from the Old Testament. In its Greek form it means literally ' what remains over,' hence, something that is reserved, after all debts are paid, as one's special possession. Like Israel before it, the Church is the treasure, the ' peculiar people ' of God. At an earlier time it was believed that in some real sense the Church had taken the place of Israel ; but when these Epistles were written the idea was understood figuratively. This is marked by the added words, **with a zest for good works**—i.e. in so far as they are resolved to do His will, Christians are God's people. Not in any exact and formal sense, but morally, they constitute a new Israel.

The chapter closes with another injunction to Titus to assert

himself boldly. **Tell them all this, exhort and reprove, with full** 15
authority. He had previously been urged to act firmly in view
of the stubborn character of the Cretan people (i. 13) ; the
reason now given is the nature of the message itself. Since
it has come directly from God, the teacher who is entrusted
with it must not be doubtful as to his right. He needs to speak
boldly, as in the name of God Himself. **Let no one slight you.**
The phrase was used in 1 Tim. iv. 12 with reference to the
youth of Timothy, and it may have the same import here;
Titus, though a young man, must not be too diffident in
asserting his authority over those who are older than himself.
But this is not expressly stated, and the thought may be
simply that Titus is to be absolutely confident of his message.
He must allow no one to question his right, knowing as he does
that he is God's servant.

THE CIVIC DUTIES OF CHRISTIANS (iii. 1–2)

iii.

Remind them to be submissive to their rulers and authorities ; 1
they must be obedient, they must be ready for any good
work, they must abuse no one, they must not quarrel, but 2
be conciliatory, displaying perfect gentleness to all men.

The Epistle has thus far dealt with the inner arrangements
of the Church and the duties incumbent on its members in their
mutual relations. The thought now turns to the obligations
of Christians as part of the larger community. Almost at once,
however, this brings the writer back to the nature of the
Church itself. How is it distinguished from the society around
it ? What is the task to which it has set itself, and which must
determine its attitude to the heathen world ? How can it
perform this task most effectively ?

So Titus is first told to **remind them** (i.e. the Christians in 1
Crete) **to be submissive** (lit. ' to be subject and obedient ') to
their rulers and authorities. In order to enforce the duty of
civic obedience the writer duplicates his words in both clauses.
Submission must be both active and passive, and authorities

of every kind must be obeyed. The Cretans were notoriously inclined to turbulence, and this was probably in the writer's mind when he laid this stress on the duty of civic discipline. But his counsel is also intended for the Church at large. For some time now Christianity had been under suspicion, and all symptoms of disaffection to the State were noted and magnified: Any resistance to authority might give the signal for a persecution which would put the whole Church in danger. It was necessary, therefore, that Christians should be particularly careful in all civic relations. Their wisdom was to give way, even when measures were taken against them which they knew to be unjust. This was no mere time-serving, but the line of action demanded by the higher interests of the Church. If it was to survive, and render its true service to humanity, it must keep clear of all political agitation.

Not only were Christians to obey authority, but **they must be ready for any good work.** This does not refer, as in previous passages (e.g. ii. 14), to acts of a specifically Christian character; it means that, when occasion demanded, Christians should be among the foremost in showing public spirit. There would constantly be outbreaks of fire, plague, calamity of various kinds, when all good citizens would desire to help their neighbours, and Christians must respond to these calls. Further, they must not be quarrelsome, but **display perfect gentleness to**
2 **all men.** Not only by actions, but by the type of character they were known to cultivate, they must show that they bore goodwill. The words **to all men** are emphatic. It was one of the grievances against Christians that they were exclusive, and too often they so interpreted the call to brotherhood as to give colour to this charge. They are here reminded that they must take up a broader attitude, if their religion was to be rightly understood.

CHRISTIANITY AS CONTRASTED WITH PAGANISM (iii. 3–8)

3 For we ourselves were once senseless, disobedient, astray, enslaved to all manner of passions and pleasures ; we spent our days in malice and envy, we were hateful, and we hated

one another. But ' the goodness and affection of God our 4
Saviour appeared ; and He saved us, not for any good deeds 5
we had done but from His own pity for us, by the water
that means regeneration and renewal under the holy Spirit
which He poured upon us richly through Jesus Christ our 6
Saviour, that we might be justified by His grace and become 7
heirs to the hope of life eternal.' That is a sure saying. 8

In the previous counsel to be helpful and conciliatory the
motive has been largely prudential. The Church is exposed to
heathen misjudgments, and by every means possible these
must be removed, since at any moment they may cause serious
danger. But other motives are in the writer's mind. He feels,
for one thing, that Christians have no right to stand con-
temptuously aloof from the society to which they themselves
so recently belonged. He feels, too, that it is their duty to
show the world what the Divine power has done for them.
They are to live among their former associates as men who have
been transformed by the work of Christ. In no self-righteous
spirit, but with a deep sense that all has come to them from
God, they are to display in their lives the contrast between
the old pagan standards and those of the new religion. The
passage is in itself a beautiful one, and historically it is of the
highest value. It helps us to understand the process by which,
in spite of all opposition, the world was won over to Christianity. For nearly a century after the death of Paul we hear of
no outstanding missionary, and yet this was the great century
of missionary progress. The whole Church was carrying on a
silent and unconscious propaganda. By simply living the
Christian life in the midst of heathen surroundings its members
bore witness to the new spiritual power.

For we ourselves were once senseless (i.e. unable even to 3
perceive a higher law), **disobedient, astray** (the image is that of
one ignorant of the road and at the mercy of every false guide),
enslaved to all manner of (diverse) **passions and pleasures.**
Two thoughts are here combined—that we were helpless
against our passions, and that they were all pulling in different
directions. **We spent our days in malice and envy ; we were**

hateful and hated one another. No doubt the writer has exaggerated the wretched condition of that pagan society to which he and his readers had formerly belonged ; but there is sufficient evidence that the picture is not untrue to fact. With the decay of old beliefs and moral sanctions, the meaning had gone out of everything. Men had nothing to live for but their own appetites, with the result that they were burdensome to each other and to themselves. Many passages could be adduced from the classical literature of the first century in which the prevailing mood is reflected, much as it is here. And in contrast to that pagan mood the writer describes the 4 awakening which had come through Christianity. **But when the goodness and affection of God our Saviour appeared.** Again we have that idea of an ' epiphany '—a sudden manifestation, which pervades the Epistles. The coming of Christ had been like a new dawn. It had brought with it the knowledge, which men could never have won for themselves, that God is gracious.

This Divine grace is described by a vivid and daring word—the ' humanity ' (lit. the ' philanthropy ') of God. This term was used by pagan moralists to denote the natural sympathy which man bears to his fellow-man. Its proper meaning is well illustrated by the only other instance of it in the New Testament : ' the barbarians showed us no little humanity ' (Acts xxviii. 2). Although the Maltese were barbarians, they were yet men, and felt pity for shipwrecked strangers. So God is here said to have sympathy with men, as men have with one another. No doubt the thought is suggested by the manner in which the revelation came—through the human life of Jesus 5 the Friend of men. **And He saved us, not for any good deeds we had done** (lit. ' not in consequence of works of a righteous nature which we had wrought ourselves.') The words are meant to summarize those many passages in which Paul declares that salvation is not earned ' by our own righteousness which is of the law ' (Phil. iii. 9) ; but Paul's meaning has not been rightly understood. The righteousness of which he speaks is scrupulous observance of the Mosaic Law, with all its ritual demands ; while the ' works ' which are here in question are those of moral well-doing. The thought is that God did not intervene to save us on account of any good in us, for in our previous days we had lived wickedly, and only deserved punishment. He saved us from (lit. ' in accordance with ') **His own pity.** The preposition is deliberately chosen. God's action was not due to any definite motive—our own deserving or even His own pity—but was simply in keeping with His Divine nature. Being the merciful One, He could not but show mercy. **By the water that means regeneration and renewal under the holy Spirit.** We are reminded of the words of John iii. 5 : ' Except a man be born of water and the Spirit.' It can hardly be supposed that the writer of the Pastorals was acquainted with the Fourth Gospel, or that the evangelist knew of this Epistle. They probably both made use of an idea which was current in the Church, and was perhaps embodied in a baptismal formula. The term here employed for the new birth is different from that in John, and was derived from the vocabulary of Stoicism. It occurs also in Matt. xix. 28, where it applies, as in Stoic philosophy, to the cosmical **regeneration** in the future : here it signifies the rebirth of the individual soul through baptism. Between this verse and the Johannine one there is the further difference that for John ' water ' and ' the Spirit ' are separate agents, although they co-operate. Here the water seems to be regarded as the sole agent. It is ' the bath of re-birth and of renewal by the Spirit.' By means of the rite of baptism the Spirit effects its work, and the re-birth and renewal are both ascribed to the Spirit. In so far as they are distinguished, the re-birth denotes the passing to a new status, while the **renewal** is the inward change which brings about this transition. A creature is born when all its members have been moulded into perfect shape. The re-birth takes place when man's nature has been fashioned anew. In both its aspects the change is due to the Spirit, which, through baptism, lifts a man out of the earthly plane to a higher one, and at the same time transforms him, so that he is in truth a spiritual instead of an earthly man.

The passage is reminiscent of 1 Cor. v. 11 : ' Such were some of you, but **ye were washed, ye were sanctified, ye were**

175

justified in the name of our Lord Jesus Christ and in the Spirit of our God.' With Paul, however, baptism is regarded as only setting the seal on the essential act of faith (cf. Rom. vi. 2–4). By faith in Christ we share in His death and resurrection, and this passing into a new life is symbolized and in some manner made valid by baptism. The writer of the Pastorals seems to think of baptism as efficacious by itself. Out of His mercy God has granted us this mysterious rite through which the Spirit works for our renewal. One cannot but feel that since Paul the Church has advanced another step towards sacramental religion. Paul had recognized a real value in baptism, but was careful to insist on faith as the indispensable condition, without which baptism was of no avail. The writer of the Pastorals conceives of the mercy of God as acting immediately through the sacred rite. In other words, the Church is now on its way towards a magical estimate of baptism, and this is evidenced by the use of what appear to be fixed ritual terms.

Yet the work of the Spirit in baptism is part of the 6 work of Christ. **He poured it upon us richly through Jesus Christ our Saviour.** The writer is true to primitive Christian thought in regarding the Spirit as given by God, but he thinks of Christ as the mediator of the gift, since it is through Him that God bestows all His kindness, **that** 7 **we might be justified by His grace.** It is to be noted that the thought here is quite different from that of Paul, although a Pauline colour is lent to it by the use of the terms ' grace ' and ' justification.' With Paul these words have reference to something definite which was achieved for men by the death of Christ. Here they apply generally to the deliverance which we owe to God's goodness as displayed in the whole Christian message. Ever since Christ came, we know God to be our Saviour, the author of all good gifts, and among them that of the Spirit, which cleanses us from evil and makes us **heirs to the hope of life eternal** (lit. ' heirs, according to hope, of eternal life '). As yet we only possess the life potentially, as an heir may be said to own the estate which is sure to come to him. Paul himself had said : ' We are saved by hope '

(Rom. viii. 24)—i.e. our salvation is still an object of hope. But when God has renewed us by His Spirit, we can look forward confidently to that eternal life which is reserved for the righteous. In a sense we have entered, even in this life, on the life which is life indeed.

The passage reminds us more of the Paul who wrote Romans and Galatians than anything else in the Pastoral Epistles ; but the outward resemblance only brings out the differences more significantly. Paul's doctrine of Justification by Faith becomes one of the Divine mercy, working constantly for our deliverance. The dying with Christ, which for Paul was the whole meaning of baptism, falls out of sight, and baptism is little more than a purifying rite. The Spirit, which Paul conceives of as the power which takes possession of the believer and rules all his thought and action, is a mysterious force which operates in baptism. So in these Epistles the ideas of Paul lose their distinctive character, and are made elements in a religion which is mainly statutory and ethical. Paulinism, while still struggling to maintain itself, is giving place to the official theology of the later Catholic Church.

Supplementary Admonitions (iii. 8–11)

I want you to insist on this, that those who have faith in God 8
make a point of practising honourable occupations. Such
counsels are right and good for men. But avoid foolish 9
controversy, and let genealogies and dissensions and strife
over the Law alone, for these are fruitless and futile.
After a first and second warning have no more to do with a 10
factious person ; you may be sure a man like that is 11
perverted ; he is sinning and he knows it.

The Epistle has been concluded by an impressive statement of the religious basis of the Christian life, but a few sentences are added to enforce once more on Titus the nature of his practical duties. There is a difficulty as to whether the formula, **It is a sure saying**, should be taken as the beginning 8 of this passage or as the close of the one before. Elsewhere it invariably applies to some concise statement, expressed in rhythmical language, which appears to be quoted from a well-known hymn or confession. Here there seems to be little that answers to these conditions, and some would understand the phrase in a general sense, ' the gospel message can be trusted.' Others have thought that it has slipped in by error, perhaps as a pious comment which someone wrote in the margin after reading the previous verses. Moffatt has adopted the view that the whole passage, verses 4–7, is quoted from some current liturgy as a ' faithful saying,' and this may be a correct judgment, though nowhere else is the formula applied to anything so long and abstract. If the reference is to the preceding passage, it more probably covers only the closing sentence. On the whole it seems best to look for the saying in the sentence following, which gives weight to the final injunctions that Titus must uphold the genuine Christian tradition in face of all efforts to corrupt it. ' Sure is the word, and that is why **I want you to insist on these things** (i.e. on all the rules and precepts which have been laid down in the course of the letter), **that those who have faith in God make a point of practising honourable occupations,**' or, ' are careful to attend to good works.' Moffatt's translation brings out, in some measure, an idea which is involved in the sentence, and may well have given it the proverbial quality of a ' sure saying.' The word ' profess ' or ' attend to ' means literally 'stand in front of,' and suggests a tradesman, diligent in business, who is always to be found waiting beside his wares. So the meaning is that religion will help you little unless you are constantly doing the actions which it requires. As the tradesman's business is to dispose of his goods, so that of the Christian is to spend his life in well-doing. His faith must be backed up with practice. One thinks of our own proverb : ' Trust in God and keep your powder dry.' The ' sure word ' here quoted would have something of the same ring to the first readers of the Epistle, although the metaphor is taken from trade instead of war.

Such counsels, as those which I have given, **are right and** good for men. He has tried, in the foregoing letter, to single out the things that are really important, alike in faith and conduct, rejecting all the side issues which bulked so largely in the false teaching. This point is made explicit in the next words : **But avoid foolish controversy, and let genealogies and** 9 **dissensions and strife over the Law alone.** We have here a recapitulation of what had been said more fully in the beginning of the letter (i. 10–16), and the Jewish elements in the Cretan heresy are again put in the forefront. Yet it cannot be inferred from this that the heresy was more Jewish than gnostic. We must remember that, while he was thinking of controversies in his own time, the author was writing in the name of Paul, and could not ascribe to Paul any definite allusions to debates that had only arisen at a later time. Here, too, as elsewhere, we get the impression that the author himself had little accurate knowledge of the heresies he denounces. He has followed the counsel which he gives to Titus, and ' held aloof ' from them, content merely to know that they were fruitless and futile. Concerned as they were with idle matters of speculation, they had little to do with the realities of the Christian life.

A sentence is added, almost casually, which perhaps **reveals** 10 one of the chief motives with which the Epistle was written. **After a first and a second warning have no more to do with a factious person.** A vague word is used (' decline ' or ' rule out '), which may apply merely to the selection of Church officers. But it has already been impressed on Titus that no man of doubtful opinions is even to be considered for any place of leadership in the Church ; and the reference must therefore be to ordinary members. Measures must be taken to keep the community entirely free from all who have a leaning to erroneous doctrine. As yet, however, the measures were comparatively mild. The offender was to be admonished, and, if he proved stubborn, was to be admonished again, and his punishment, in the last resort, was not to take the form of expulsion, but only of leaving him out of account. He must be made to feel while he was still nominally a member he had no real part in the Christian fellowship. Perhaps the passage in Matt. xviii. 15–17 on the treatment of the erring brother was in the writer's mind, and is applied to one particular kind of error. Heresy was not yet a deadly sin, but only a grave fault, which might be corrected by persuasion and discipline.

It is in this verse that the word 'heretic,' in something like its technical sense, appears for the first time. Originally it meant simply 'one who takes sides,' especially in some religious or philosophical dispute, and no suggestion of blame was involved. But the idea of party connected itself naturally with that of the factious temper, and already, in Gal. v. 20, 'heresy' is coupled with enmity, strife, division (cf., too, I Cor. xi. 19). It is possible that the word 'heretic' is here used in its earlier sense of 'partisan,' and that the injunction applies to any ill-tempered people who create discord in the Church ; but the previous verse seems to point definitely to those who divide the Church by accepting false doctrine. This 11 is further indicated by the reason given for rejecting the **factious person** who is obdurate : **you may be sure that a man like that is perverted** and sins. His stubbornness shows that the evil has taken a real hold on him. He has not fallen into his error inadvertently, but is wilfully blind to the truth. To reject him, therefore, is no act of arbitrary judgment, for he is self-condemned. Since he cannot be moved by better counsel, he must be sinning against the light. He knows that he is wrong, and his own conscience endorses your sentence.

Personal Notices and Greetings (iii. 12–14)

12 When I send Artemas or Tychicus to you, do your best to come to me at Nicopolis, for I have decided to winter 13 there. Give a hearty send-off to Zenas the jurist and 14 Apollos ; see that they want for nothing. Our people must really learn to practise honourable occupations, so as to be able to meet such special occasions ; they must not be idle.

In this closing section a genuine fragment of Paul's correspondence may be preserved—a hasty note for the direction of Titus or some other of his assistants. To be sure, nothing is known of a sojourn of Paul at Nicopolis, but he only speaks of an intended visit. If Paul wrote the note (and the language is entirely in his manner), he must have sent it at some time during his stay at Ephesus, or when he had passed over from Ephesus to Macedonia and was still in doubt as to whether he would be permitted to spend the winter at Corinth. The mention of Apollos precludes a date before the Ephesian period, and shortly after that Paul had finished his missionary career.

When I send Artemas or Tychicus to you. Of Artemas 12 nothing is known from the New Testament, but, according to tradition, he became bishop of Lystra. **Tychicus** is mentioned in Acts xx. 4 as one of the Asian delegates who accompanied Paul to Jerusalem, and he appears prominently in Ephesians and Colossians as the messenger entrusted with those letters. It is indicated in the present passage that Titus is shortly to be relieved by Artemas or Tychicus, but Paul is still uncertain as to which of them he will send. **Do your best to come to me at Nicopolis, for I have decided to winter there.** Of the several cities called **Nicopolis** ('city of victory'), the most likely is that which was founded by Augustus in Epirus, to commemorate the battle of Actium which made him emperor. It was famous as the home of Epictetus, who taught there shortly after the time of Paul. **Give a hearty send-off to 13 Zenas the jurist and Apollos.** Nothing is known of **Zenas,** who is called a lawyer—perhaps to distinguish him from another Christian worker of the same name. He may have been a former Jewish scribe, but from his Greek name it is more probable that he was still, or had been, a practising lawyer. **Apollos** is well known from the book of Acts and 1 Corinthians. It has been conjectured that these two men were the bearers of the present letter, but Apollos, almost from the first, was one of the foremost teachers of the Church, and could not have been spared for subordinate duties. Here, indeed, we seem to have evidence that this fragment at the end was artificially attached to the letter, for if Apollos had gone to Crete he would have taken precedence of Titus as a missionary and would not suddenly appear in this casual fashion. We get the impression that Paul is writing to secure honourable entertainment for two eminent teachers. When their visit is finished, they are to be escorted some way on their further journey, with due care taken that they want for nothing—i.e. they were to be supplied with provisions and everything else they might require.

This request that the comfort of the visitors should be properly seen to is made the ground for a general counsel, introduced, it would seem, by the author of the Epistle into the genuine note by Paul. The peculiar phrase 14 which Moffatt translates practise honourable occupations has evidently a reference to the ' sure word ' which was quoted in verse 8. It there applied to the diligence in action by which Christians must give proof of their faith in God, and has doubtless the same meaning here. Our people (i.e. we Christians) must really (or rather, ' must also ') learn to make themselves practically useful. It would seem to be implied that Christians were commonly regarded as dreamers, whose religion unfitted them for the ordinary duties and courtesies of life. The writer acknowledges that there is some truth in this opinion. Too often when a visitor said good-bye to a Church prayers were offered for his welfare on the journey, but no one thought of ensuring that he should be suitably clothed and fed. Christians must learn to be at least as assiduous as their pagan neighbours in attending to such ' necessary requirements.' Moffatt may be right in understanding this phrase to mean special occasions, but more likely it only refers to bodily needs. Travellers on a long journey could not be expected to live wholly on prayers and good wishes. The thought of the ' faithful saying ' is again touched on in the words, they must not be idle (or, more literally, ' unfruitful '). In so far as faith does not have its outcome in good action, it has gone for little.

CLOSING SALUTATIONS (iii. 15)

15 All who are with me salute you.
   Salute those who love us in the faith.
   Grace be with you all.

As usual in Paul's letters his fellow-workers join with him in the final greeting, which Titus is asked to convey to **those who love us in the faith.** The suggestion may be that some of the friends who join in the greeting are personally unknown to those who are in Titus' company, but that **the** common faith is a bond which makes all Christians brethren.

From the closing benediction, **Grace be with you all,** it is clear that the letter, though personal, is meant to be communicated to the whole Church. Or perhaps this general benediction belongs to the Pauline fragment, and is out of place in the personal letter to which it has been appended.

INDEX